ON
EAGLE'S
WINGS

ON EAGLE'S WINGS

*The True Story of the
Founding of Eagle Boys' Ranch*

JOHN VARDEMAN

Published by
Looking Glass Books
219 Woodlawn Avenue
Decatur, Georgia   30030

Manufactured in the United States of America
ISBN 0-9640852-2-4

On Eagle's Wings is published in honor of Loyd Strickland,
whose early commitment to the Eagle Ranch
dream helped make it a reality.
— *Friends and family of Loyd Strickland*

Acknowledgments

The idea for *On Eagle's Wings* grew out of the 1991 Board of Directors retreat and the Directors' desire to record God's blessing of the Eagle Ranch ministry for present and future generations.

We were fortunate to have in our midst John Vardeman, a tremendously talented writer. When approached about this ambitious project, he quickly "volunteered." What began as a short, factual history of the Ranch grew into a book that I believe even took John by surprise. Over the past four years, he has worked tirelessly in developing this book and, as a result, has provided an account of God's provision for Eagle Ranch in an inspirational framework.

Countless people will be touched because of John's sacrificial giving to this project.

We would be remiss if we did not acknowledge and thank John's wife, Tracy, who was very supportive throughout this whole process and was without her husband many weekends as he labored on the book. We also are grateful for the hard work that Jean Parks, Eagle Ranch's administrative assistant, put into transcribing John's interviews with Eddie Staub and others, working out the book's timeline, and editing. Many thanks also to our publisher, Dick Parker of Looking Glass Books, who took this project on with a passion and whose commitment to excellence mirrors our own.

There are many other individuals without whom this book could not have been written, especially those who gave their time for interviews and provided their unique perspectives on these events.

Finally, a special thanks to all of those who have helped make the Eagle Ranch dream a reality. Be assured your giving has been used by God to provide for some very deserving children — now and in the future.

In closing, none of us associated with the Ranch have any illusions that Eagle Ranch could have ever existed apart from the powerful working of God's hand. It is indeed "the miracle on Chestnut Mountain."

To God be the glory!

Jerry Keen, Chairman
Eagle Ranch Board of Directors
1995

Contents

Prologue

January 1992

Banquets and such affairs of high society ranked high on his list of least favorite activities. He always felt a nagging pinch of uneasiness and isolation among people who mingled as if they had known each other since childhood. Exacerbating his discomfort was his height. He towered a good five inches above six feet, making it difficult to camouflage his presence among a uniform backdrop of suit coats and gowns. The extra elevation nearly always exposed him.

This night, however, wasn't that bad. He had a passing acquaintance with at least a few of the men and women coursing between the white-tableclothed tables of the main banquet hall at the Chattahoochee Country Club. Furthermore, they primarily numbered in age from twenty to the early thirties. That qualified him, from the perspective of his own thirty-six years, as practically an elder. It helped to relax his tenseness, though he still would have preferred a pair of faded jeans to the constraining formality of a cotton tie around his neck. Given a choice, he also would have opted to spend this particularly cold Friday evening at home with his wife and two children. With such tremendous demands at the office, every minute at home was a precious gift. At least tonight, the man thought, his wife was with him. Too often he had to fulfill these obligations on his own.

Following the cue of a select few who began seating themselves at a long, rectangular head table, the audience of young professionals slowly divided into parties of three couples, claiming separate tables for the duration of the night. The man and his wife fell in step with the couple who had invited them. Together with another husband and wife, they settled down at a table already adorned with small plates of salad and a cloth-covered basket of rolls. The sight was a welcome one, for the man had pre-empted lunch that day for two stressful noontime meetings. Had the cocktail conversation around him not been so blaring, he was certain his growling stomach easily would have been overheard. Just in case, he quickly stuffed a few bites into his mouth, hoping to allay his embarrassment before the crowd hushed for the invocation. Fortunately, the moment of silence did not occur until midway through the entree.

Before bowing his head, he glanced at his wife, who already had leaned forward and closed her eyes in prayer. Her dark black hair was suspended in front of her, shielding her face from either side. He felt himself wanting to sneak a better view. She looked especially beautiful that night in a simple yet sophisticated patterned evening dress that was rarely worn. On his modest income, along with her primary responsibilities of raising the children, she did not often experience such elegant affairs. Since he had been invited to the dinner, this outing was free; still, it pleased him to feel somewhat responsible for treating her that night.

The Young Man of the Year banquet, which was hosted every year by the local Jaycees service organization, was a prestigious affair in Gainesville, a prosperous, outer-metropolitan community northeast of Atlanta, Georgia. The long list of award winners dated back to the 1950s and included several men who had gone on to become national and state leaders, bank presidents and other highly successful businessmen. All award winners were invited back to the banquet each year; most could be spotted easily by the telltale tops of their heads, which were either balding or graying.

Keeping with local tradition, the identity of each Young Man of the Year was a secret closely held by a small selection committee composed of honorees from the previous five years. Consequently, the conversation at most tables — as it did every year — inevitably came around to speculation over the night's award winner. There were numerous obvious guesses that fell in line with the profile of previous selections: a banker or lawyer who had headed up that year's successful United Way drive or perhaps presided over a high-profile committee of the local Chamber of Commerce. A good blood-line was helpful, too — someone who had grown up in the community with a last name synonymous with the tradition of "old-line Gainesville."

Following dinner, the suspense had to wait another half-hour while an incumbent Georgia congressman talked about patriotism and current political affairs. By the time local banker John Byrne, the previous year's Young Man winner, approached the podium to announce the honoree, the evening already was approaching 10 p.m.

The audience hushed in anticipation. Several tables back from the podium, the man momentarily let go of his wife's hand and drew his own to his mouth to suppress a yawn. He was getting restless. His wife patted him on the back and smiled warmly. She smiled partly out of love — and partly because she knew something that he did not.

The speaker turned his head to clear his throat, then moved back to the microphone to begin his introduction. "This year's recipient is not a native of Gainesville," he said, keeping the riddle intact for the moment. "He only moved here ten years ago, but since then he has made an enormous contribution to this community and all of Northeast Georgia."

In the audience, a few privately self-proclaimed candidates re-laxed, immediately ruling themselves out, a little disappointedly, from the running. By the early sound of it, this year's winner would not conform to the usual trend.

"He came from a small community outside Birmingham, Alabama, where he went on to Auburn University and earned a baseball scholarship. ..."

In the audience, the man looked around in curiosity. Surely, he thought, he must know this fellow Auburn graduate, particularly someone who played baseball there like he did. His eyes met his wife's and he noticed they were pooling with wetness. Unable to pretend any longer, she took his hand and squeezed it lovingly. And all at once he knew. He immediately hung his head, tremendously embarrassed, and listened to the rest of his story.

"... Our Young Man of the Year knew no one and had next to nothing when he first arrived here," the speaker continued. "All he had was a dream — a dream to build a boys' home for this area which so desperately needed a local facility with services for troubled children."

With that statement, most of the audience now knew the answer, and the man began to feel their stares. He continued to look down at his feet, flustered and surprised over what was unfolding.

"In the end, this man accomplished his impossible dream because he believed in himself and in his Creator. His desire and his heart can all be summed up in a motto that hangs on the wall of his office: 'Attempt something so great for God that it is doomed to failure unless God is truly in it.' And so he did, and — with God's help — so he succeeded, too, in building what is now the largest home for needy children in Northeast Georgia and one of the most progressive in the country — such a success story that CNN television news has dubbed it 'the miracle on Chestnut Mountain.'

"With his unique collection of skills and talents, this year's Young Man of the Year recipient could well have been a vice president or CEO of a successful business. But, speaking for this community and the many young lives whom he has touched, we're certainly thankful that he followed his calling to our door instead.

"Please, everyone, join me in recognizing this year's Young Man of the Year — Mr. Eddie Staub."

Tables and chairs scuffed the floor noisily as the audience rose to its feet in heavy applause. The man stood slowly and a little weakly, still shaken by the surprise. He turned and received a long hug from Kayanne, his wife. Someone reached out and gently nudged him toward the front of the room, where the speaker waited with a new name engraved on the gold plate of an old wooden plaque.

Eddie Staub ambled his way awkwardly toward the front, shaking several hands along the way. As the plaque was placed into his hands, he felt the first twinge of emotion building in his chest. However, it was not the award that moved him; it was his sighting of a young man smartly dressed in blue military garb. He stood so far in a back corner of the room that no one had noticed his entry. No one would have recognized him anyway or even been aware of the magnitude of his own accomplishments: a standout in basic training at Lackland Air Force Base in Texas and a top pick for Officer Candidate School, where he had further excelled two years earlier. After continuing to impress his superiors with an acute technological proficiency in electronic warfare, he had been selected, once again, for promotion. Most impressive, however, was from how far down he had risen to achieve his present standing. Only the thinnest trace of a scar in the left corner of his mouth gave a clue to the former depths of his pain-wracked life. His and Eddie's eyes locked on each other as the crowd quietened and awaited the customary remarks from the honoree. Eddie stood silently, feeling like an impostor on center stage. This award doesn't belong to me, he thought, still staring at his friend whom he had not seen for several years. There's the real hero, he wanted to say out loud. There in the back of the room is your real Young Man of the Year.

Still unseen by the majority of the back-turned audience, 1st Lieutenant Rodney Hudgins stepped forward a few inches to gain a direct line of sight through the crowd of heads. His lips trembling, the young man slowly raised a hand to his brow. He stood frozen for several seconds in a salute of paramount respect, his eyes never wavering from the civilian at the podium.

To Eddie, it was without a doubt his greatest honor of the night.

"Even youths grow tired and weary,
and young men stumble and fall.
But those who trust in the Lord for help
will find their strength renewed.
They will soar with wings as eagles."

Isaiah 40:30-31

I

MOUNTAIN BROOK

Chapter One

July 1966

The first pitch was a strike.

Eddie Staub, batting for the third time that night, hung his head in a moment of despair. Then, emulating his make-believe big brother, Rusty Staub of the Houston Astros, he tossed his hand in the air, signaling to the umpire for a time-out. He stepped back from the plate, went to one knee, and scooped up a sandy handful of Alabama dirt.

The big "ump," by far the largest form on the field at around 250 pounds, swatted at a mosquito buzzing in the vicinity of his square crew-cut head. Two dark wet spots spread under each arm of his blue uniform shirt and already crept halfway down the side of his barrel chest.

"Okay, kid. Let's get on with it. We ain't got all day," he spat with a gust of impatience. At ten dollars a game, his enthusiasm eroded with each motion of the home-plate ritual.

The eleven-year-old batter was a bit taller and skinnier than most of his teammates; otherwise, he looked no different from the average Little Leaguer in the average little town. Still, he was considered among the best, at least in Mountain Brook, where coaches routinely selected him as one of the top picks in the annual Southern League draft. That summer of 1966, it was the Braves — maybe not the greatest among the community's young boys of summer, but the blue-jerseyed team suited Eddie Staub just fine. Besides, he was more interested in the trappings of his favorite sport. That's why he played catcher. The position had more pads and contraptions than any other on the field.

"Ball!"

One and one. Eddie still hadn't taken a swing. Like they said on those late-night WWL Radio broadcasts from the Houston Astrodome, "he was looking for one up in his wheelhouse." Eddie imagined himself in all the radio baseball clichés. He was a "disciplined hitter." He could "dig one out of the dirt" if he had to, or "sacrifice himself for the team" if it meant "moving a runner into scoring position."

Eddie dug in again, tapping his wooden bat to the plate for position, then glanced once more to make sure the "Louisville Slugger" trademark was turned away from harm. The feat of cracking a bat pivoted between hero and goat. A bat broken in combat was the sign of a near home run, the kind of power exhibited by Hank Aaron on those muggy summer nights at Atlanta Stadium. But if the splinters revealed a direct hit to the trademark, the Little League batter suffered a fate no less dreaded than death by firing squad: humiliation by peers.

"Steeeeee-r-r-r-r-r-i-i-i-i-i-i-k-k-k-k-k-k-e!"

Again, Eddie had watched the ball buzz by. The wooden stands behind home plate erupted in laughter. Eddie sneaked a sideways glance, fearing his stoic turn at bat might be tickling the crowd; but their attention was latched instead on the umpire, another major-league-wanna-be.

"Think your son knows it was a strike?" someone in the bleachers said, softly nudging the batter's father, Edwin John Staub Jr., with an elbow in the side.

"Windy really does get into it, doesn't he?" he replied.

The next pitch was high. "Ball," whispered the umpire. Only strikes and outs excited the big man, known to most parents in the bleachers simply by his blustery nickname. To Windy, pitches way out of the strike zone merely prolonged his agonizing crouch behind the plate. The count was now two and two. Respecting Windy's waxing impatience, Eddie quickened his usual round of preparations before crouching back over the plate for the next throw.

It was a forty-five-mile-per-hour fast ball, and this time it spun right up to the front door of Eddie's wheelhouse — chest high and outside. His swing met the ball smoothly on the sweet part of the bat, the place where a batter hardly feels the impact. Only the bat's loud crack and his own instincts let Eddie know he had knocked a big hit to centerfield.

It all seemed like a slow-motion dream. His chin tucking into his chest as he sprinted to first base, Eddie hadn't even noticed the ball's long-distance flight until he was halfway to second. Player No. 9, the lanky leftfielder, hoisted himself high atop the outfield fence. Perched a few inches from the ground and balancing on the horizontal silver-metal bar with two locked arms, the boy watched in amazement as the ball skipped through the pine trees on the other side before disappearing into the wooded darkness.

Prior to Eddie's swing, no one in all of Mountain Brook's roster of Southern Leaguers that season had lifted a pitch over the Park and Rec's chain-link fence at John Black Field. No one, either, would do it again that year. But on this day, Eddie's day, he had sent the ball "downtown."

As Eddie sprinted for third, he looked back across the infield and began to feel funny. The other players were silent, motionless statues, their mouths agape and their backs all turned to home plate. "Hey, Eddie, slow down! It's a home run!" a teammate yelled from the Braves dugout. But Eddie didn't. He ran across home plate and straight to the dugout. Maybe because he was so shy. Or maybe because he knew he had gotten lucky. For whatever reason, he just didn't want it to be such a big deal. But it was.

"Wooooooooooooooooo! Ya-hooooooo! Way to go, Eddie! The big home run king!" shouted his teammates, forgetting for the moment that they still trailed 3 to 2. They whacked him on the back over and over so hard that he felt he might lose his breath.

In the stands, Eddie's father sat quietly, very much amazed but proud nonetheless. He leaned in different directions to shake hands, nodded at each congratulatory wave, and fielded his own share of back-slapping.

"Can you believe it?" said Jim Stewart, a co-worker of Ed Staub at Alabama Power. "He hit the daylights out of that thing!"

"Well, he sure surprised me, too," Eddie's father said. "I didn't know he had it in him."

Jim began to stroke the shadow of whiskers on his chin, and his smile slowly receded. "You know, I've always told you there's something special about your boy. He just proved it to me again, right now, with that home run."

"Well, thank you."

"Sure. But I'm really not talking about his hitting per se. Your son, … uhhh, let's see … how should I say this? Don't take this wrong … Eddie's a good ballplayer, but he really had no business hitting that ball out of here — nor anyone else in the Southern League for that matter. That fence is way too far out there."

"How do you think he did it then?" Ed Staub was still seated, though everyone around him was standing. He waited a few seconds for an answer, then turned to look up at his colleague.

"That's just it," Jim said, squinting his eyes as he searched for Eddie in the dark shadows of the home-team dugout. "I'm not sure I can put my finger on it. But like I said, there's something special there, something different. That's all."

Chapter Two

Fort Benning, Georgia

The baby boy had been crying for what seemed an hour. His sixteen-year-old mother's face was streaked with tears. Tears of frustration. She had tried everything. A pacifier. The bottle. Nothing was working, and she was running out of time.

Soon — very soon — her husband would be home. And she was scared. Scared for herself, and scared for little Rodney.

Chapter Three

Less than a month had passed since Eddie's big home run, and already the memory of it was fading. For Eddie, there was always a whole lot more to look forward to than to remember — especially in summertime.

For the moment, it was horses. Mom had announced a few days before that Dad was taking the family out to the riding stables on Saturday. The days had passed slowly, like waiting for Christmas morning, but finally it was the night before. Eddie gobbled his second helping of tuna casserole as if eating faster might coax the kitchen clock on the wall to pick up the pace. Friday-night fish was a weekly regimen at the Staub home, as was characteristic of most Catholic families. Much of Eddie's young life revolved around the typical — all wound up in a clockwork schedule of sameness and rituals. Mass on Sunday mornings. Bedtime every night at nine, right after his prayers. Chores every day during the week, though the list was pared down during the school year. And then Saturdays. Saturdays were for kids. For playing sports. For riding bicycles. And especially for riding horses.

Day after day in Mountain Brook was the only life Eddie and his two younger brothers, Billy and Bobby, had ever known. By fifth grade, Eddie had lived in three different houses — he only remembered two — but each was within only a few miles of the others. A suburb of Birmingham, Mountain Brook was among the most affluent communities in the country, and Eddie's family, though far from being considered wealthy by Mountain Brook standards, enjoyed a comfortable lifestyle nonetheless.

Ed Staub was employed with Alabama Power as assistant manager of industrial development for the entire state. But perhaps because of his pauper roots in the ministry — he had very nearly become a Jesuit priest after twelve years of seminary — the Staubs lived a conservative and disciplined life at home. Love was the only exception. For while the words "I love you" rarely were uttered out loud, it was an unspoken emotion that was displayed in overwhelming abundance.

"Hey, Dad, since I'm oldest, can I have first pick of the horses tomorrow?" Eddie asked, flashing a big grin at youngest-brother Bobby, then at middle-brother Billy.

"Eddie, I think the three of you should be old enough to work that out for yourselves," his father said. "But we'll need to get an early start tomorrow, or there'll be nothing left but the grades."

The stables' grade horses were the least-desirable picks for riding. They didn't seem to have the spirit and smarts of the full-breds, like Eddie's two favorites, Bobba Luie and Silver.

"Okay, boys, enough talk about horses," interrupted Teleete Staub, Eddie's mother. She waved a finger in mock disapproval. "No one's going anywhere until you help me clear this table."

Eddie's father winked, then stood up from his chair at the traditional head of the table. "Eddie, why don't you sweep the floor for your mother."

"Yessir," he answered in the universal Southern tongue of respect spoken between son and father.

Eddie curled his big hands around a well-worn, red-handled broom and meticulously brushed the floor in a precise pattern that ended several minutes later in a small dust pile in the middle of the room. Like his father, he took pride in performing even the most menial of tasks with perfection. He was applying the final strokes, kneeling with the front page of Thursday's newspaper in one hand and the broom handle choked up in the other, when his father returned. "Nice job, son. I know your mother appreciates it."

"Hey, Dad, wanna play a little Pepper?" Eddie asked, referring to his favorite front-yard sport of fielding baseballs batted by his father.

"Well, all right. You go get everything and I'll meet you outside."

"Yessir!" he exclaimed, returning the broom to its proper post, then running upstairs to collect his bat, ball and two gloves. The evening was closing down toward eight o'clock, but a good hour of daylight and dusk still remained. Daylight Saving Time would see to that.

Eddie lived for the approval of his father. And he knew his dad's reluctant acceptance to join him in a good three innings or so of practice was a tacit expression of satisfaction. Whether sweeping the floor or cutting grass, Eddie seldom cut corners in trying to please his father. It was an ambition rooted in love, for Eddie's father rarely had to resort to the feared rubber-worn Ping-Pong paddle to keep his boys in line.

With Billy, Bobby and Mom inside watching TV, Eddie and his father began warming up with short pitches between them while gradually backing up to a more respectable throwing distance. The limbering of muscles was much more for father than son — Eddie was loose enough from twenty or more innings that day with his friends at the Park and Rec ballfield.

Eddie's father dropped his glove to the ground, picked up the bat lying at his feet and propped it on his shoulder. It was a signal for Eddie to assume his imaginary shortstop position. For the next forty-five minutes, Eddie snagged every grounder and pop-up that came his way. Eddie did most of the running, maneuvering into position with each hit and chasing the occasional ball that shot past him into the neighbor's yard. But as darkness began to settle in, it was his father who stuck out his tongue in mock exhaustion. "Eddie, you've just about worn me out, and you're going to get hit in the head if it gets any darker. I think it's time to get ready for bed."

Eddie didn't want to quit, but he followed his father without protest. "Thanks, Dad," he said after they were inside. "What time do we have to get up tomorrow?"

"I'd say we better shoot for eight. That'll give us a good hour-and-a-half to get ready and make the drive out to Shannon Stables."

"Eddie, you and your brothers need to get out your riding clothes before you go to bed," his mother said, entering the front hallway as Eddie and his father pried off their grass-stained tennis shoes.

"Yes ma'am."

"I'm surprised you guys quit your throwing so early," she teased. "There must be at least another five minutes of daylight out there."

"It was Eddie," her husband retorted. "You know how exhausted he gets out there. He can hardly keep up with me." Eddie grinned. He started to say something back but switched attention to his two brothers who were skidding across the floor toward him in their sock feet. Their TV show over, the pair was looking for some entertainment from Big Brother.

"Okay, gang. Everyone upstairs to bed, or we'll be sleeping too late to make it to the stables on time," their father commanded.

✝ ✝ ✝

As Eddie closed his eyes on another day of summer vacation, he couldn't imagine being any happier. There was horseback riding in the morning, and — in a few weeks — the promised trip to Atlanta to visit Six Flags amusement park and watch the Braves at the stadium. Surrounded by the love of his family and an equally blessed life outside his door in Mountain Brook, it was hard for Eddie to imagine life from any other perspective. That night, if there was another child somewhere out there who hungered, who longed for the love of his parents, who longed for his very own baseball bat and glove, Eddie had no cause to wonder who or where that child could be.

Chapter Four

The oldest and youngest had drawn their two favorite horses at Shannon Stables. Eddie sat atop Bobba Luie, a beautiful jet-black steed. His seven-year-old brother, Bobby, had nabbed the other favorite, Silver, a young blond filly. Billy Staub had settled for last pick, grabbing the reins of his pathetic-looking nag like a warrior challenged with a dropped gauntlet. The nine-year-old was determined more than ever to show up his brothers, especially after they teased him with the name, "Mr. Nag's Head," in honor of his less-than-desirable mount.

"Now, boys, be careful," their father warned from the other side of a fence. "And remember — no racing."

In perfect unison, the young trio of musketeers nodded their assurances, twitched their knees, and snapped their reins, slowly nudging their horses across the open field toward a sign-posted trail. Inside the cover of woods, the two older brothers yelled out a chorus of commands and simultaneously slapped their horses into a gallop. Bobby feigned a similar effort, bellowing out a loud whoop but not digging in his boots nearly as hard. He was still skittish about horses.

Eddie calmly directed his streaking steed through the brown-needle path, occasionally slapping his cheek against the outreached branch of a pine tree. After a few minutes, he stole a glance behind him and smiled. No one in sight. He pulled up gently on the reins, and the horse answered like a private to a sergeant, smoothly slowing down to a leisurely walk before coming to a full stop. The horse let out a raspy snort as Eddie turned the animal sideways in the path. He waited. Thirty seconds later, he spotted his youngest brother and horse trudging toward him in a slow gait.

"Where's Billy?" Eddie called out.

Bobby twisted his head to look down the path, then turned back around. He smiled triumphantly. "I guess I lost him!"

"Or maybe the Indians got him. We better circle back around and see if he's okay. Dad said we need to stay together," Eddie said, firmly assuming the big-brother role.

Eddie felt a small pang of guilt. Their brother, Billy, had been good-natured enough to go with a nag, and they had left him behind. ... Or had they?

"Wait, Bobby. How do we know he's behind us? Even if he was on foot, he should have caught up to us by now," Eddie said. "I'll bet he took the loop road and is trying to head us off. Maybe he really wanted that grade horse after all. That way, if he passes us, he really makes us look bad. We'll never hear the end of it! Come on!"

Eddie jerked the reins sharply to his right and resumed his original course. Bobby laughed, nearly falling off his horse, and followed in step behind his big brother. The early-morning sun was starting to pierce through the trees, warming the air. The heat already had both boys sweating a bit, so the cool air that greeted them as the horses regained speed was exhilarating on their sun-tanned skins. They charged up a small knoll, crossed a trickling stream on the other side, then sprinted down the home stretch toward a fork in the path where they half-expected to find their grinning, gloating brother.

"Whoa, Bobba Luie!"

"Whoa, Silver!"

Bobby steered his filly next to Eddie's horse, and the two boys fell silent. They listened to the stillness. The high-pitched chatter of katydids, a squirrel shaking a leafy tree limb, and a mourning dove singing its refrain. But not one sound or sight of Billy and his horse.

"Well, we've gone way too far to turn back now," Eddie said, his face showing concern. "Let's head on to the field."

The two brothers coaxed their mounts again, this time with a great deal more trepidation. Billy was probably all right. But Dad wouldn't be pleased that they had gone off and left him.

They cleared the woods a few minutes later, and what they saw on the other side of the field was a sight that the family would laugh about for years. There was Billy, still saddled on his nag near the site of their journey's first step a half-hour earlier. He was kicking furiously and yelling something. But the nag showed indifference, finding much more interest in a dew-moistened clump of grass at the base of a fence post. The animal swung his head of matted brown hair into the green-grass salad and came away with another munchy mouthful.

"Billy, where have you been?" Eddie called out, half-knowing the answer.

"Right here!" he responded, his frustration breaking through. "I haven't moved from this stupid spot the whole time, except when this stupid horse finds something else stupid to eat!"

Eddie put on a sympathetic face and tried to think of something to say. But he was distracted when, out of the corner of one eye, he spied his father on the other side of the fence wearing the thinnest trace of a grin and slowly shaking his head. All three brothers turned at once toward their father and stared in wonder at his rare display of amusement. Then, one by one — as if on cue — Eddie, Bobby, and even Billy, broke loose into three toothy smiles.

Chapter Five

Rodney no longer was crying, but his mother was. She looked again at the purple-red bruises on her son's neck and sobbed even harder. But not too loud. She didn't want to wake her husband.

At the other end of the trailer, Sergeant Jack Hudgins was passed out on a sofa, mumbling between snores. He always seemed to snore loudest after a night of heavy drinking. Sally Hudgins stepped back from the side of her son's crib and stared vacantly into the black darkness where her husband lay. If she had a gun at that very moment, she might have used it. But then where would she be? Neither she nor her baby would be any better off, especially with the loss of a military man's income. Had he broken Rodney's neck? It was possible. The child seemed to lie so still. So quiet. So helpless.

An hour ago, around 2 a.m., Rodney had finally settled down when his father slammed open the trailer's metal door. Startled out of his half-sleep, Rodney had begun crying again. Then his father, still dressed in uniform, had stumbled to the crib and screamed back at his son, positioning his face only a few inches from Rodney's as if dressing down a new Fort Benning recruit. The crying only worsened, and that's when he lost all control. He put his hands around the baby's neck and began to press — harder and harder until the child could not breathe.

The sudden silence had scared Sally so much that she, too, had gone berserk. She scrambled across the trailer into her son's room and let fly a torrent of fists against the back and neck of her husband. The distraction finally caused him to release his hold, but the ugly fight that followed had left her with a black eye and a sprained arm. She had torn into her husband like a wildcat and was lucky to have suffered no worse injury.

Sally cringed now as she remembered Rodney's crib slamming against the wall during the scuffle and nearly turning over. She peered back at her motionless son, too scared to touch or move him. Through the murkiness of her tears and the room's dim glow from a night light, she searched for some sign of life. Her heart quickened as she saw something flicker. Rodney opened his tiny brown eyes and blinked. She watched quietly, then sighed in relief as her little baby boy stared back. His look of desperation, she thought, seemed to mirror her own.

Chapter Six

Sunday mornings followed a routine around the Staub home. This one, like most, was sunny outside and busy inside as the family hurriedly showered, combed and dressed up for Mass. Eddie looked into a mirror and worked on his tie for the third time. He knotted the thing every week, but it always seemed to come out too short the first time, then too long on the second try.

Eddie wanted to look sharp — even if it rarely got him anywhere with the girls at Mountain Brook High. He was now a junior. He had his driver's license and his own red '67 Camaro. Still, he had not mustered the courage to ask even one girl out on a date, despite the fact that a few had asked him to be their escort to a couple of high school dances. There was still hope, though — and even if church rarely offered any candidates, he always wanted to be ready.

The disciplined work ethic preached by Ed Staub to his three sons carried over into the family's church attendance and spiritual life. Eddie couldn't remember missing even one Sunday Mass in his entire life. The Staubs attended church even on the annual family vacation to Panama City Beach, Florida. There also were the Bible lessons imparted unknowingly under the cloak of father-son talks when Eddie or his two brothers had been caught egging a neighbor's house, talking back to their mother, and pulling off innumerable other acts of adolescent rebellion.

Eddie finished adjusting his tie, finally getting the two ends to match up just right over his belt. He left his room and walked downstairs, where he found his father sipping hot, black coffee while scanning the Sunday paper.

"Morning, Dad."

"Good morning, Eddie."

His father was a quiet man — and especially so in the morning. Eddie understood and did not attempt to extend the conversation. Without a word and without looking up, his father held up the sports section of *The Birmingham News*. Eddie took the handoff and plopped down at the breakfast table to check the major league box scores from the previous night's baseball games. Together, they waited in silence as the rest of the family trickled one by one down the stairs and into the kitchen. A few minutes later, they filed into the family car and were on their way to church.

The road to St. Francis Church was lined with tall pines and a majestic array of homes proclaiming the town's neatly groomed mix of old and new wealth. Watching the moving scenery from his backseat car window on the way to Mass, Eddie mused over how Sunday mornings always seemed to highlight Mountain Brook's best face. He closed his eyes, almost dozing, and continued to picture the peaceful street whizzing by outside. Every corner of his hometown, from its ballfields to its bike paths, was neatly folded and tucked inside his memory — like precious flowers pressed between the pages of a book. He would leave Mountain Brook one day. But his hometown would go with him.

✛ ✛ ✛

Eddie's nose was buried inside the St. Francis Church bulletin, so deep that he didn't notice her at first. The little girl's parents waited until most of the congregation were seated before rolling her in her wheelchair down the aisle to the front row.

The silver-haired priest, Father Pat Michael, stepped to the pulpit and announced a page number. A loud crackling noise bounced off the church walls and filled the cavernous room as the crisp white pages of several hundred song books were snapped and turned all at once. The pipe organ whistled to life, beseeching the congregation to sing along.

Before the first verse was completed, Eddie's eyes already were straying from his hymnal and scanning the pews. Song time was always a good opportunity to search for the occasional pretty blonde or brunette.

Finding no prospects among the forest of gray-haired elders, Eddie started to open his mouth for the refrain. Then he saw her, a dark-haired girl poised in silent prayer within the stark confines of her wheelchair. She sat next to the end of a pew, only a few feet from the altar. Wearing a plain white dress, she looked like a little angel — except that her wings had been replaced with two black-rubber wheels. Eddie's heart burned and his eyes quickly moistened with tears. His emotion surprised him, but he couldn't help it. He felt so deeply sorry for the girl. "Why?" he thought to himself. "She's so young. *Too* young. How could anyone — especially a child — deserve to go through life like that?" Had he not been in church and in the middle of a hymn of praise, Eddie might have blamed God. Anger and finger pointing always helped numb the pain of remorse.

Throughout the remainder of the service, Eddie could hardly keep his eyes away. He forced himself to focus on the pulpit, but it did no good. He could not stop looking. The girl was like a magnet, and every stare hurt him as badly as if someone had punched him in the ribs.

As the service ended and the congregation filed from the pews, Eddie briefly considered approaching her. But his shyness — and an overwhelming feeling of futility — froze him in his seat. At that moment, Eddie uncovered something about himself, but he was too overwhelmed by his emotions to comprehend.

God had blessed him with many gifts. All-American good looks, athletic ability, a loving family, and this spontaneous emotion that had surfaced so unexpectedly — it was a gift, too. A curiously special gift. Eddie possessed a deep and caring burden for those who hurt, those faced with an unhappy life. On that beautiful Sunday morning in Mountain Brook, in a church and a community so surrounded by God's riches, Eddie could not yet understand the blessing behind his private torment. Someday, he would.

Later that night, when Eddie retired to his bedroom, he still had not shaken his anguish. Dressed in a pair of plain white boxer shorts, he knelt down beside his bed and clasped his hands in prayer.

"Lord, please help that little girl that I saw today at Mass," he prayed silently in the darkness of his room. "Help make her life a little better somehow."

Eddie prayed almost every night, alone and without anyone's knowledge. At school, he was president of the local chapter of the Fellowship of Christian Athletes and an active member of Young Life, a Christian ministry to high school students. He didn't smoke or drink, and he rarely said a cuss word. Still, none of his classmates, even those with a propensity toward the wild side, viewed Eddie as super religious or a goody two-shoes. In this way, he was much like his father, displaying an easily likable example for his peers while saving his greatest intensity for his private faith in God.

Eddie finished his prayer and rolled into bed. He stayed awake for at least another hour, his mind continuing to race with thoughts of the little wheelchair angel. When he finally fell asleep, the angel followed him into his dreams.

Chapter Seven

The day Eddie stepped onto the campus of Auburn University, his mind was consumed with one devoted passion — earning a baseball scholarship. He knew his parents were right when they said to put his studies above everything else. But, in this rare instance, Eddie had decided to put their advice on the shelf for a while. As long as he made C's and B's, and as long as there was enough light in the day to practice, he would focus on baseball.

There had been a few opportunities for scholarships at smaller schools, but Eddie wanted Auburn. All his life, he had been a War Eagle, and all his life, he had been a baseball player. Now he intended to see the two finally come together.

Auburn's junior first baseman, David Laramy, first noticed Eddie during the third week of practice in the spring of 1974. Laramy was well aware of the extra hoops that a walk-on athlete at Auburn had to jump through. He had been one himself before earning a starting position on the team, and he knew that every walk-on, if worth his salt at all, had to work extra hard to catch the coaches' attention. "But this Staub guy," Laramy thought after the first few days of drills, "he's practicing himself to death!"

Laramy had finished his shower one late afternoon at Auburn's Memorial Coliseum and looked forward to a rare night away from the athletes' dining hall — a thin-and-crispy pepperoni pizza out on the town with the boys. An hour earlier his lungs had been on fire from wind sprints. It was the team's toughest practice in recent memory, and Laramy hoped he never saw another one like it. He walked to his car and slung a canvas gear bag into the open back seat of a blue Chrysler convertible. He stopped and cocked his head. In the distance, he thought he could hear the faintest sounds of someone panting and straining. Dusk was settling over Auburn's campus, so he had to squint hard to spot the lone figure on the practice field.

Laramy shook his head in disbelief. "That's gotta be Staub. I ain't believing this guy," he said out loud to himself.

He paused, looked at his watch, then started walking toward the field to check out this idiot for himself. Eddie didn't notice him approach until Laramy opened his mouth.

"Geez, Staub. Lighten up!" he said. A thin, teeth-clenched smile stretched across his face. "You'll never make the squad if you kill yourself first!"

Eddie popped out of his catcher's stance and threw sharply to the net at second base. He turned and nodded at Laramy.

"Oh, hi. How's it going, David?" His voice was weak and out of breath.

"How's it going? It's going out for pizza and then home to bed — that's where it's going. How 'bout you? You gonna stay out here all night?"

Eddie pulled off his glove and wiped the sweat from his brow. "Nah. I was just finishing up."

"Why are you doing this to yourself, Staub? The coaches have all gone home. I'm the only one around to impress — and I just think you're crazy."

"Listen, I'm not trying to show off. I'm just trying to make the team. And I've got a lot of things to work on if that's ever going to happen."

Laramy's face broke into a bigger grin and his nostrils snorted. "Say, did I see you out here before practice, too?" he asked.

"Uh, yeah. I guess it was me."

"Jumping rope? Push-ups? Sit-ups? That kind of crap?"

"Yeah. Just trying to keep myself in shape."

"Hey, Eddie."

"What?"

"That's what regular practices are for."

Laramy waved a hand in mock disgust and turned to walk back to his car. Halfway there, he spun back around.

"Hey, Eddie!" he yelled while continuing to walk backward up the small hill leading to the coliseum parking area. "All I'm saying is just don't kill yourself. You gotta learn to pace yourself, or you'll burn out!"

"Okay, David. We'll see ya later."

Eddie waited until he heard Laramy's car drive off. He crouched down in a batting stance, threw his arms into an imaginary swing, then launched himself into a series of all-out dashes around the bases. The night was pitch black by the time he rounded third for home for the last time.

✢ ✢ ✢

Ed Staub had watched his son toddle with a plastic bat and ball at age three. He had coached him and played games like Pepper with him in the backyard all the way to suppertime and through Little League and junior high. He had attended as many of Eddie's high school games as work would allow. And now, here he was, in the stands watching his son in an intrasquad game at Auburn University.

No one could have seen or detected the stirring of emotions tucked behind Ed Staub's stone-like gaze. But it was a powerful and proud moment for him. His son was a better-than-average catcher and already seeing a little playing time off the bench, though most of it in games when either Auburn or the opposing team had posted a comfortable lead. With a little more playing time and a lot more luck, Eddie just might win that scholarship. Eddie's heart was set on it; Ed hoped his son would not be disappointed.

Ed Staub's job at Alabama Power continued to require a large portion of his waking hours, and together now with the increased number of miles between him and his oldest son, it had become even more difficult to keep in touch. His heart sometimes ached when he thought about how fast all three of his sons were growing up — and how decreasingly little time he had to share with them.

He watched his son stride to the batter's box and go through the motions of preparation that had become so familiar after more than ten years of watching. His son was nineteen years old now and had developed into quite a good-looking catcher — tall and muscular with a crackerjack throwing arm. That day, Eddie swung a pretty good bat, too. He went four for five in addition to throwing out all three runners trying to steal second base.

Ed Staub's presence always seemed to bring out the best in his son. Eddie's mother, Teleete, often joked that her husband should take a leave of absence from work during college baseball season and go on the road with Eddie. Funny, funny. But, oh, how he would have loved to do just that.

After the scrimmage, Eddie took an evening off from his post-practice routine to join his father for dinner. They drove a few miles off campus to Morrison's cafeteria, one of Eddie's favorites, where he knew he could count on a good home-style meal of bread, fresh southern vegetables, fried chicken, and sweet iced tea.

"You looked good out there, son."

Eddie grinned. It was the best feeling in the world to please his father. "Thanks, Dad. Coach Nix said they might redshirt me next season — give me time to work on my hitting. Hope that means they're thinking about giving me a scholarship."

"Eddie, I know I've told you this before, but you need to pay more attention to your books. Baseball's not always going to be there for you, but a good education stays with you for the rest of your life."

"Yessir."

A waitress stopped at their table, prompting a momentary break in their conversation as she set a big pitcher of iced tea on their table.

"There you go, sir," the woman said with a wink. "That'll save me the trouble."

Eddie thanked her, then turned back to his father, who wore a look of mild curiosity.

"They know me pretty well around here, Dad. I guess they'd rather give me a whole pitcher of tea rather than walk back over here every five minutes."

Ed Staub chuckled, then furrowed his brow as if to remind his son of the serious nature of their discussion. "Eddie, have you thought about what you plan to do with your life?"

"Well, I don't really know yet. I've been thinking about pre-med. But my grades haven't been too hot in chemistry."

"What type of medicine, son? A pediatrician? A sports doctor, maybe?"

"Well, I really haven't thought that far ahead, Dad. I guess…" Eddie paused, mustered up his confidence and looked directly into his father's eyes. "I guess for now I want to keep practicing hard at baseball. Because, who knows? Maybe I could play professional ball someday."

Ed Staub opened his mouth to respond but was interrupted.

"I know, I know," Eddie said, holding up his hands. "That's something I can never count on."

Eddie's father smiled. He didn't want to press his son too hard, but he did want him to do a little more thinking about life after baseball. "Well, you've still got some time to sort through things. But you're right about one thing. You can't count on baseball."

"Yessir."

The remainder of their conversation provided Eddie with the usual updates on the Staub family — Mom, Bobby, Billy, and his grandparents. Little had changed and Eddie was hardly interested, but he listened politely.

"Well, son. This being the middle of the week and I do have to be at work early tomorrow morning, I guess I better head home. It was good to see you."

Ed Staub extended his hand and Eddie clasped it with his own — a quick but heartfelt handshake.

"You, too, Dad," Eddie said, noticing a slight feebleness in his father's grip. Ed Staub was diabetic, a fact rarely mentioned by Eddie or anyone else in the family. But it was a concern that rumbled faintly in the back of Eddie's mind like a dark and distant cloud.

"Dad, you've been feeling okay lately?"

"Oh sure, son. I'm just a little tired. Ready for the weekend, I guess, so I can wear myself out with all the odd jobs around the house."

"Take care of yourself, Dad."

"You, too. Eddie. I'll try to make it back to another practice game — or maybe a real game — later on this season. I'd like to see another one of those 'four-for-five days' like you had at the plate today."

Eddie would, too. And only a few minutes after his father drove away for Mountain Brook, Eddie's mind was back on baseball.

Chapter Eight

In many ways, Eddie Staub had lived an extended childhood. The Vietnam War had wound down by the time he turned draft age, and calm finally prevailed over the riots of Alabama's desegregation days. With so few distractions from the outside world, Eddie had filled the void with games. There was mostly baseball, but also horseback riding, touch football on the campus grounds, and plenty of flirting and dating — the latter of which had seen a significantly higher batting average since high school. Toward the end of his sophomore year in April 1975, however, Eddie's life in the sun was about to darken. The first storm clap sounded with the ring of a telephone.

"Eddie, you've got to come home."

"Mom," Eddie said, holding his breath. "It's Dad, isn't it? What's wrong?"

He sat up in bed. The digital alarm clock read 10:34 p.m. Eddie had been asleep for nearly half an hour, but a surge of adrenaline jolted through his body like ice water.

"Yes, Eddie," his mother answered. "His health has taken a turn for the worse. He's gone into renal failure. They've rushed him to St. Vincent's." Her voice sounded soft, but amazingly calm.

"I'll be there in two hours. Mom, are you okay? Is someone driving you to the hospital?"

"I'm already here, Eddie, with Bobby and Billy. So don't you go speeding down the highway. Be careful."

"I will, Mom."

"Promise?"

"Yes, ma'am."

It was one of the few times Eddie ignored his mother.

✢ ✢ ✢

Teleete Staub stood with her three sons outside the intensive-care unit at St. Vincent's Hospital in Birmingham. The doctor spoke in such a hushed tone that Eddie, Bobby and Billy had to lean forward in a strained collaborative effort to hear. Their mother, though, hardly seemed to pay attention. Her steel-blue eyes were cloudy and ringed underneath with heavy dark lines.

"What did he say?" she asked after the doctor left.

Billy, now a senior at Mountain Brook High, opened his mouth to explain but was interrupted by his older brother.

"Dad's gone into a coma, Mom, and they're going to move him into a private room," Eddie said in a strained but authoritative voice.

Billy glared scornfully at Eddie but held his tongue. Their mother sighed and nodded her head.

"I think they've done all they can for him, Mom."

"I see."

"At least he's not in any pain," Eddie said.

"Can we go see him?" she asked wearily.

"Not yet. They've got to run a few more tests and stuff. It might be best if we all go home and get some sleep."

It was two in the morning, and they were all exhausted. Neither Eddie, his mother, nor his two brothers had left the hospital in the last twenty-four hours — except for brief walks outside to escape the stuffy antiseptic air. Eddie's youngest brother, Bobby, had returned to his makeshift bed on a couch in the waiting area and was already asleep.

"Okay, son," Eddie's mother said. "I almost hate to wake Bobby again, but he'll feel better in the morning if he sleeps in his own bed."

Billy moved quietly to Bobby's side and kneeled down. "Come on, Bobby."

"Huh? What?" Bobby said fuzzily as he tried to focus in the semidarkness of the waiting room.

"Come on and get up. You haven't been asleep that long," Billy said. "We're going home."

Several minutes later, Eddie took his mother by the arm and the Staub family — minus one — strolled to the elevator and outside to the car. During the twenty-minute drive home, no one said a word.

✢ ✢ ✢

The next morning, Eddie felt a little fresher, even if his spirits were still dampened by the sight before him. His father lay motionless, his eyes closed, under the crisp white linens of a hospital bed. A nurse had inclined the bed so that Ed Staub sat at a sixty-degree angle. Eddie hardly recognized him, so ashen and puffy. He hoped that when his father died that he would remember him the way he used to be — not like this.

Bobby and Billy were still at home asleep. The plan was to let them stay out of school that day and visit their father around lunchtime. Eddie and his mother had decided to take the first shift, arriving by seven that morning. An hour later, Teleete had left her husband's room and walked down the hall to the hospital chapel. Adorned with a crucifix, stained-glass windows and the other familiar furnishings of church, the tiny prayer room had provided Teleete with the only steady ground amid her shaky, clinical surroundings. She had been its most frequent visitor in the last two days.

Eddie took his father's left hand in his own and squeezed it. There was no response. The only sign of life now was his chest. Covered beneath the sheets, it seemed to barely lift the spread with each small breath. Eddie noticed the time between breaths also had seemed to grow longer.

Without closing his eyes, Eddie began to dream in the sterile stillness of his father's room. He watched himself grow up and his father grow old. They were outside the house in Mountain Brook, throwing and hitting a baseball; as usual, Eddie was wearing out his father. Then they were in Panama City, sitting on the beach, watching the waves crest and roll toward their beach chairs. Now he was atop his favorite horse. He saw his father on the other side of a fence. Eddie waved, and his father smiled. He waved back at his son, and then faded away. So many happy, precious times together — they all seemed to have lasted as briefly as it took to remember them.

Eddie left his imagination and found himself beside his father again. Their lives together had come full circle, but Eddie believed the circle to be too small. He leaned closer to his father and held his breath to hear his father's own. Finally. He saw the chest move up, then down. But barely.

Moving his head even closer to his father's, Eddie whispered, "I love you, Dad." He couldn't remember the last time he had said those words out loud to his father. He sat back in his chair and waited again for his father's next breath. But this time, it never came. Eddie stood up and stared down at the body of his father. Leaning over the bed, he kissed him on the forehead, then stood back up, struggling not to cry. He had to be strong. He had to get ready to walk down the hall and tell his mother what the doctors had told them would happen. Ed Staub, the greatest father who ever lived, had passed away.

Chapter Nine

The Auburn campus — often described as "the loveliest village of the Plain" — looked very different to Eddie when he returned from his father's funeral to finish spring quarter 1975. Jordan-Hare Stadium, quiet for the moment between football seasons, looked venerable as ever from its corner of the campus. Beautiful green lawns seemed to sprawl forever while hundreds of pink and white azaleas outside an array of classroom buildings neared the end of their bloom cycle. Between classes every Monday through Friday, the campus sidewalks gushed with laughing students. All of it, the entire campus scene, was still there like before — only it now appeared stark and in black and white. Despite Eddie's pain, life went on at Auburn University, and the indifference seemed to mock him like some callous bystander.

For the first time in his life, Eddie felt entirely on his own, with no one to look after him but himself. Without his father, he had decided to take charge of his life and, to the chagrin of his two brothers, that of his entire family, too. Eddie would try to take control of everything around him. He had bossed his two brothers to the point that they hardly spoke to him. Without realizing it, Eddie was attempting to replace his father — for his mother, for Billy and Bobby, and for himself.

Baseball became his whipping post. It was no longer a game like he had known in Little League or in the backyard with his father. He relentlessly threw all of his fears, his anger and aggression into the sport.

He left himself no time for grieving. Classes began at eight in the morning and lasted till noon. There was no break for lunch, for Eddie worked at the athletic dorm, serving meals until 1:30 p.m. The rest of the day went to baseball. Push-ups, sit-ups and jumping rope for an hour, two-and-a-half hours of regular practice, and another hour afterward.

By the end of the 1975 baseball season, Eddie's hard work was finally paying dividends. His intensity in practice sessions was spilling over into his play on the field, and Auburn Coach Paul Nix had noticed.

Exam time neared as Auburn's baseball team wound down its regular-season schedule. The year had been a good one and, although the club had not won the conference championship outright, there was still hope for the playoffs.

Another Monday afternoon practice session was almost underway with Eddie sweating it out well before his teammates had donned their uniforms and left the locker room. His last sit-up completed, he began a round of slow stretching exercises. An intrasquad game was scheduled at three-thirty, and Eddie wanted to be loose.

By the time he stepped up to the plate for his first turn at bat, he was ready. Swinging on the first pitch, Eddie clipped a clean single to right field. The hit was only his first of an amazing six-for-six day at the plate. Eddie played his best intrasquad game of the season, battering the ball as if it were a grapefruit and throwing out all four runners who attempted to steal.

Eddie and his hard-work habits no longer were the fodder of jokes among his teammates. His sweat had finally earned their respect, and when the game was over, his teammates crowded around him in a genuine display of admiration.

A week later, Eddie received the news from Coach Nix that he had earned his long-awaited scholarship. The announcement came not with fireworks or cheering but was heralded rather innocuously with the ringing of a telephone while Eddie visited his mother at home in Mountain Brook.

"Eddie, if ever anyone earned a scholarship the hard way, it was you," Coach Nix said on the other end of the phone line. "Congratulations."

"Thanks, Coach. I really 'preciate it," Eddie responded.

Their conversation was brief. Eddie heard the click and dial tone in the phone receiver, then stared blankly at the den wall. It must have been that last intrasquad game that I played so good in, he thought to himself. I knew something good had to come out of that.

He daydreamed back to the week before. There he was, surrounded all over again by his teammates, feeling proud and embarrassed at the same time as they laughed and slapped him across the back. During the celebration, Eddie remembered how someone had flipped up the bill of his cap, sending it spiraling backward off his head.

Standing now, with the phone receiver still in his left hand, he remembered kneeling down to retrieve his hat and noticing the old wooden stands on the third-base side. A few rows up was where his father used to sit when he came to watch Eddie play.

The seat was empty.

Chapter Ten

Rodney Hudgins spat a gritty piece of rock from his mouth, then tore back into his latest adversary. He punched hard with his right into the stomach of little Johnny Volhein, following with a solid left to the face. Johnny's nose and face ruptured in a mixture of blood and tears. His knees buckled and he fell backward onto the playground's crushed gravel.

Rodney leapt forward to finish him off but was abruptly yanked upward by his shirt collar by Jim Reynolds, the assistant principal at DeKalb Elementary. "All right, that's quite enough," he said. The kicking and clawing second grader hung helplessly in the man's strong grasp.

An older woman with a bun of blue-gray hair, one of the two teachers on Thursday playground duty, moved swiftly to the fallen victim's side. She pulled a wadded-up napkin from her purse and pinched it to the nose of the crying boy.

"There, there now," she said in a soothing tone. Then, turning with a glare toward the boy's junior assailant, the woman forced her voice down an octave. "You again, Rodney?" she said. "Why is it always you?"

"They were making fun of me," Rodney shot back. "Calling me a 'whale-fair' boy."

The pressing crowd of elementary kids slowly pulled back. None of them quite grasped the meaning or pronunciation of "welfare," but they figured it must be a bad word. A few turned and ran just in case Rodney started pointing fingers.

"Okay, off to the office, Rodney," Mr. Reynolds said, sounding as though he already had passed judgment. "Mrs. Gilbert, does the boy seem okay?"

"Looks like he was lucky this time," she answered. "Just a bloody nose. Might have been worse, though, if we hadn't gotten here when we did."

"But they were all making fun of me!" Rodney said. His voice cracked and he began crying.

"Not me!" the bloody-nosed Johnny Volhein said, breaking his wounded silence. "I was just a-standing here, not doing a thing."

That was doubtful, Mr. Reynolds thought to himself as he rubbed his forehead. Give 'em credit, though. These second graders can be awfully good actors. Who really knew how the fight started? All he had to go on was Rodney's brief history, and it wasn't a good one. Rodney had a nose for trouble, and this time he had sniffed up a little too much. His mother would have to be called in on this one, though he doubted it would do much good. She was … well, just what the kids had said — a welfare case.

Rodney Hudgins and his mother, Sally Hudgins, had moved to Decatur, a small city in the suburbs east of Atlanta, during the previous spring of 1976. She was a recent divorcée, having finally mustered the courage to walk away from an abusive husband after eight years of a stormy marriage. Her ex-husband was miles away now at Fort Benning, Georgia, and his only clue to her place of refuge was an Atlanta post-office box number. But in the back of her mind, Sally knew that he would find her sooner or later — and that someday he might come after her, or after her boy.

Sally and Rodney lived in a tiny apartment off Rocky Ford Road in Decatur. A relative who lived in the area, her Aunt Betty, had found the place for her, and for the first six months, Sally had done pretty well for herself with an assembly-line job at a local cannery. But orders at the plant gradually slowed until layoffs became inevitable. As one of the newer employees, she was among the first to go.

Now she worked part time as a convenience store clerk and had recently started drawing welfare. The infrequent child-support checks from her ex-husband had stopped appearing altogether in her post-office box. Turning to federal assistance had been a final act of desperation. Sally's parents had turned their backs on her long ago, when she had decided to marry at age fifteen. There was nowhere else to turn. She had too much pride to approach her Aunt Betty or more distant relatives. Welfare had become her anonymous benefactor.

For the first few months of food stamps, Sally had found it easy to hide her indignity among a metropolis of nearly two million strangers. But it wasn't long before the kids at school caught on — particularly after Johnny Volhein's mother explained to him about the strange-looking coupons that Rodney and his mother used to buy food one Saturday morning at a Decatur grocery store.

The heckling on the playground had started soon afterward. Rodney wasn't too sure what they were talking about, but he fought back anyway. His latest scrap was the third in as many weeks.

Sally Hudgins had just returned to her apartment when the phone rang with the news about her son. The assistant principal asked her to drive over immediately for a parent-teacher consultation.

"Mr. Reynolds, can't we just talk about it when I come to pick up Rodney after school?" she asked him over the phone. "I've got so many errands to run this morning." She was job hunting.

"Mrs. Hudgins, I'm afraid this is not Rodney's first fight. He has become very disruptive, and I must insist that we discuss this matter as soon as possible."

"Can we schedule it after lunch?"

"That will be fine," he answered. "I'll see you in my office at one o'clock."

"One o'clock. Okay, I'll see you then."

✝ ✝ ✝

Sally walked through the front door of DeKalb Elementary — twenty minutes late — and found Assistant Principal Jim Reynolds talking on a phone in a reception area just outside his office. He was surrounded by several teachers wearing worried expressions.

"Mrs. Hudgins?" he asked, cupping the phone receiver with his free hand.

"Yes, I am. Where's my son?"

"I'm sorry, Mrs. Hudgins. I was hoping he was with you, but I'm afraid now that he may have run away."

"What! Where is he?"

"After we talked on the phone, Mrs. Hudgins, I gave him permission to eat in the lunchroom," the assistant principal explained calmly. "He was told to report straight back to my office after lunch, but apparently he never made it to the cafeteria. One of our teachers, Mrs. Earhart, tells me she saw your son running down Trinity Street outside the school. He's been missing for about an hour now."

Chapter Eleven

Rodney turned off busy Ponce de Leon Avenue and began walking down Lullwater Road. Behind him, he dragged a stick he had found on the sidewalk. He had passed by the street's stately old mansions many times in a car with his mother, but until now he had never realized how big the homes really were.

It had been two hours since he slipped away from school, so he figured they must be looking for him by now. Dropping his stick, Rodney left the sidewalk to scale an ivy-covered wall surrounding one of the Lullwater mansions. On the other side, he found a huge old oak tree with big broad limbs — a perfect place to hide and watch for bad guys, he thought.

Rodney quickly scooted up the tree, using its weather-worn crevices as toeholds. Several vines draped around the tree's massive trunk, providing excellent ropes to pull himself up. For a brief second, he wondered if he could tear away one of the vines and swing through this enchanted forest like Tarzan of the Apes.

He climbed as high as he had ever climbed a tree, and still he figured it wasn't even halfway to the top. Looking down, he felt a tinge of fear. But he found safety in a broad limb that curved down about a foot before branching up to the sky — the perfect perch! From his guard tower, Rodney could spy down on his prisoners below, and no one could see him tucked away so high and deep in the heavy green foliage.

An hour had passed before Rodney started to ponder how he would end his great escape. He was already bored and a little disappointed that he hadn't spotted any search teams scouring the woods below him. Maybe no one knew he was missing yet. Or maybe no one cared.

A sleek, black BMW pulled off Lullwater, stopping at the driveway entrance below Rodney's roost. He watched as an older boy he recognized from school stepped out of the car and pulled a bundle of letters and magazines from a mailbox. The car door snapped shut again, and the vehicle drove up the steep driveway to a garage with a door that opened automatically.

Rodney wondered what it would be like to live in a castle like this one. The front windows of the home were too dark to see inside, so he could only imagine what was on the other side — probably servants and maids and an indoor swimming pool. The surroundings below him seemed so foreign — and so strange that they could exist so close to his own little apartment home and his own school. Rodney was too young to understand that time and distance had less to do with royalty than social class and birthrights.

Rodney's stomach growled. He was getting hungry, and the day's light was beginning to fade. Better start climbing down now, he thought to himself, before it gets too dark to see. The descent was more difficult than the climb, and Rodney slipped and scared himself a few times on the way down. By the time he reached the ground, darkness had turned out the lights around him, and the castle before him began to twinkle with its own lights. Rodney thought it looked kind of like that Walt Disney World place on TV.

Back on the sidewalk, Rodney headed toward the busy main street of Ponce de Leon. Still unsure of where he was going, he wandered through a large, grassy park where several people still milled about, jogging or walking their pets.

Rodney stopped at the sight of a crusty, scary looking old man hunkered over a metal trash can. One of the man's arms was completely submerged in the receptacle, fishing around for food scraps and spare aluminum cans that could be turned into money.

Rodney walked past the old man, then turned around to stare. I wonder if he's a "whale-fair" person like me, Rodney thought.

A hand suddenly clamped down on his shoulder, and Rodney twisted away in panic. Before he could escape, however, an arm followed from the other side, wrapping around his waist and hoisting him in the air.

"Hold on there, fella." It was a policeman.

The uniformed man set Rodney gently back down on his feet, then bent his knees until he and the boy were at eye level. "What are we doing walking around here this late at night?"

"I don't know," Rodney answered, shrugging.

"You wouldn't happen to be Rodney Hudgins, would you?"

"Yeah," he said slowly, unsure of the consequences. "That's me."

The police officer stood up and pulled a radio from his belt. He turned on a static noise, and Rodney heard a crackling voice that he couldn't understand. The noise stopped as the officer pulled the box to his mouth.

"Station, this is Hendricks. I found the boy."

Chapter Twelve

Teaching science and physiology at Campbell High, with a student body half the size of Mountain Brook High School, was not exactly Eddie's picture of the perfect job. But it was a good start.

Eddie had graduated from Auburn that summer of 1978 with a degree in science education — and absolutely no pro offers from the major leagues. Of course, by then he hadn't expected anything more, for Eddie had finally let go of baseball. It started during the middle of his junior year. Something had begun to churn around inside him until it finally bubbled up to the surface. Once it did, he never recovered. Someday, he might go back to examine exactly how and why it all happened, but for now he pushed it way back to the darker-most edges of his mind.

The transition to life after baseball had been difficult, if not agonizing. But Eddie was growing older, and with age had come greater maturity and confidence. His growing independence had germinated several years earlier with the loss of his father; the end of baseball stripped him of yet another crutch.

Eddie now saw baseball from a different angle. In addition to his teaching duties at Campbell, he was the school's head baseball coach. He was happy to still have a hand in the sport that had touched so much of his life, and he especially enjoyed molding the young players on his team. Still, Eddie couldn't help thinking there was something more to strive for in his life. He guessed he just hadn't found it yet.

Campbell High School lay south of Atlanta in Fairburn, a small town near one of the nation's busiest airports, Hartsfield International. The jet traffic over his practice field reminded Eddie of watching a New York Mets home game on television; pitchers on both fields had to learn to concentrate with the overhead roar of 737s constantly buzzing over their heads.

Although Campbell was only a few miles from a major urban center, the school still had a small-town feel. However, with a black student body of about thirty percent, it was a world apart from all-white Mountain Brook High. Many of the students also came from a much lower socioeconomic upbringing.

The exposure to a less fortunate strata of life served to rekindle some of Eddie's confused feelings for people who weren't given the same security and comforts that he had growing up. His burden for the hurting may have been in hibernation for a while, but he had never forgotten the pain he felt as a young teenager upon seeing the meek little girl in a wheelchair that day at St. Francis.

During his second year of coaching, his scar was reopened at a baseball game between Campbell and Feldwood high schools. This time, the source of his pain bore no wheelchair or obvious physical impairment. In fact, the kid was very athletic — the cleanup hitter for Feldwood. Eddie never learned the boy's name, only that he lived at a children's home in nearby Union City, Georgia. But like the impressionable experience with the girl in the wheelchair, he thought about him for days.

As he did, an idea began to roll around inside Eddie's head. Intertwined with the emblazoned image of the anonymous boy from the children's home was a burning desire to lend a hand to others like him.

Back at Mountain Brook High, he had once met a young charismatic and inspirational man named John Croyle, who had spoken at a Young Life gathering. Croyle was a former All-America defensive end under Coach Paul "Bear" Bryant at the University of Alabama. He also was the founder of Big Oak Ranch, a three-year-old nondenominational Christian boys' home for needy children outside Gadsden, Alabama, Croyle's hometown. Eddie had always admired Croyle. He even credited Croyle, a tremendously talented speaker, for leading him down the path toward becoming a Christian during high school. If anyone could help Eddie sort through his aspirations to work with needy children, it was John Croyle. He was the man who might provide some answers. On a lark, Eddie decided to call him one night on the phone from his apartment in College Park.

Several minutes into their conversation, Eddie felt embarrassed and more than a little regret for having called. Croyle sounded too busy to talk. Eddie began thinking of a graceful way to exit. Then, out of the blue, came the unexpected. Croyle invited Eddie to visit Big Oak to allow them to meet and talk in person. Flattered by Croyle's sudden interest, Eddie jumped at the offer.

Wasting no time, Eddie scheduled a meeting for the coming weekend. He was overdue to visit his mother anyway, so he planned to pair the Big Oak meeting with a trip back home.

✢ ✢ ✢

As he sat in John Croyle's office, Eddie felt an instant kinship with the man on the other side of the desk. Conversation came easily between them, and Croyle seemed genuinely concerned over Eddie's restless pondering of the future.

"Eddie, there's only one way I know for you to figure this thing out," Croyle said. "Come to Big Oak and work with me for a summer. That way you'll learn whether it's what you need to do or not."

For the second time in a week, Croyle's off-the-cuff manner took Eddie by surprise. The invitation to work with someone of his reputation was a great opportunity, and Eddie had to bite down hard to mask his excitement.

"I'd like that, John," he said. "But let me think about it for a while, and I'll call you back."

By the time he left Croyle's office and turned his car onto the main road outside, Eddie had already made up his mind. A few months later, at the end of the school year, he would pack his bags and head for Big Oak Ranch. It was a venture into the unknown that would begin to change his life — and that of many others — forever.

II

BIG OAK RANCH

Chapter Thirteen

Summer 1980

"Welcome to the Big Oak Hilton," said John Croyle, banging open a screen door with a broken spring.

He amusingly searched Eddie's face for a reaction. They were standing at the stoop of a small, two-room cabin, Eddie's living quarters for his summer experiment at Big Oak. Streams of broken sunlight peered through a dusty window. It provided just enough illumination for Eddie to see the dirt foundation between the slightly warped boards of the wooden floor.

"Looks wonderful," Eddie replied, smiling back at his new boss. "Just like home."

John laughed. He had known from their very first talk on the phone that he would like this Staub fellow. Now he was even more convinced. "Tell you what. I'll help you get all your bags in. You get everything settled; then come next door, and Tee and I'll fix you a nice steak for dinner — compliments of the Hilton."

"Ummmm. Sounds like a winner," Eddie said.

Eddie's car was unpacked in minutes, and John walked next door to prepare for dinner. There was no phone in the cabin, so John had said he'd holler out the window when they were ready. Eddie sat back in a rickety recliner covered in cheap velvet-like material in the cabin's main den area. Had it not been so hot inside — there was no air conditioning — he probably would have fallen asleep. Eddie was worn out from the drive from Fairburn.

This place is worse than a summer camp cabin, Eddie thought. But the primitive nature of his indoor surroundings actually helped him feel much closer to the bucolic beauty outside his door. Big Oak was 120 acres of peace and quiet — at least on his side of the lake. Two 3,600-square-foot homes — holding up to eight boys each — sat across the eight-acre lake outside Eddie's door. One was a metal A-frame structure. The other was a brick home and much nicer in appearance. The rest of the grounds consisted of rolling hills, dense woods of mostly pine trees, a second lake covering five acres, and two large fenced-in pastures where several cows and horses grazed. It all seemed like the perfect place for a young boy to escape and forget his troubles.

Eddie finished unpacking, then relaxed his tired muscles with a lukewarm shower. At least the place had running water, he thought. Afterward, he reached into an old, scratched-up chest that had lost two of its drawers. He retrieved a pair of jeans and a fresh T-shirt — formal dinner attire for Big Oak Ranch.

The bunkhouse was still warm from the Saturday afternoon sun. Eddie feared he might start sweating and present an ugly first image for John and his wife, so he stepped outside to cool off.

A moment later, John waved from the front door of his small two-bedroom home.

"Come on over and help me grill these steaks, Eddie!"

Eddie jumped off the stoop and jogged the short distance to his new neighbor. Inside, he said hello to Tee Croyle, John's wife, whom he had met earlier that day.

"Glad you could make it, Eddie," she said sweetly. "We're looking forward to having you here at the ranch."

"Thanks, Tee. I'm happy to be here."

"Are you sure?" she asked, reaching inside an oven to poke three foil-wrapped potatoes with a fork. "You haven't changed your mind after seeing what John calls the Big Oak Hilton?"

"Nah," Eddie answered. "I think I'm going to like it. It's got real charm."

"Well, maybe someday we'll be able to afford a little better accommodations for our staff," she said. "The boys here are our top priority."

"I understand."

John Croyle pushed open a door from the other side of the room. "Coals are about ready. How do you like your steak, Eddie?"

"Oh, whatever. I don't eat it enough to know any better."

"Okay, we'll make it medium-rare then. Three juicy-pink steaks coming right up."

Later, over dinner, Eddie asked his hosts to tell him how they had started Big Oak Ranch. He had heard and read bits and pieces of the story before, but never from Croyle himself.

"Well, Eddie, if I hadn't messed myself up playing football, I might never have gotten around to it," John said, winking at his wife. "You know that I had serious knee injuries in my senior year at 'Bama. There still were a few offers from the pros to try out as a free agent, but my heart wasn't in it. I felt the Lord was calling me to start a children's home instead.

"I had some experience working with Dave Simmons' camp in Mississippi for several years back in college. You remember him … used to play linebacker with the Cowboys."

John put his hands behind his head and stretched out his six-foot, six-inch frame. "I believe God's given me the gift to communicate and help children who need help. And my connections to the coaches at 'Bama and Auburn haven't hurt. Fund-raising is an important part of my job here."

"John, you should really be proud. I've heard nothing but great things about Big Oak," Eddie said.

"Well, thanks. But we've still got a long way to go. We've got two homes with houseparents in both, and we've got a social worker who helps counsel the kids and keeps our records updated for the state. Right now, we're housing about sixteen boys, but I'd like to see us build up to forty kids or more in the next year or so."

Boys between the ages of six and eighteen were referred to Big Oak from Alabama's Department of Family and Children Services as well as from private sources. The cases ranged from child abuse and drugs to neglect and abandonment. The ranch provided these unfortunate children with a chance to start over, surrounding them with a stable Christian family atmosphere and filling their days with a busy schedule of farm chores and school.

"Eddie, some of the boys that you're going to work with this summer may trouble you," Croyle said, leaning forward in his chair for emphasis. "They come from situations that make the Big Oak Hilton seem like the lap of luxury."

"I'm sure," Eddie answered.

"Some of their stories will shock you and make you want to cry. So be prepared," Croyle said.

"John, why don't you tell Eddie about some of our boys?" Tee said, jumping into the conversation. "Tell him about Peter."

John looked down at the floor and took a deep breath. "Peter is real special. Came to us about a year ago after his mother threw hot grease on him in a fit of anger. Only seven years old. His chest scars have about healed now, but there's still a lot more healing to go on the inside. He's got a lot of emotional problems."

Eddie grimaced and felt a wave of compassion for this boy whom he had not yet met.

"Then there's Charlie, who was banished by his parents to a dirt basement for several days of punishment. They fed him by shoveling food down the steps to him on the ground like some sort of animal. He still has nightmares about bugs and spiders crawling all over him."

Eddie noticed Tee's eyes beginning to moisten. She undoubtedly had heard the stories before, but they apparently never stopped hurting her.

"Two of our saddest stories here at Big Oak are Chris and Jimmy. They're twins, and they'll be starting second grade this fall," John continued. "We got them only a few months ago from the state. They never knew their father. Their mother is a prostitute, and she simply doesn't want them around anymore. Apparently, she works out of her home and having kids around is bad for business.

"Anyway, despite all that, these two little boys adore their mother. They literally starve for even one tiny drop of her love and attention. During their first day at the ranch, they tried to run away three different times to find her.

"A few days later, they came into my office crying and begging to see their mother. It broke my heart. So I gave in and called their mother for them on the speaker phone — worst thing I could have done. She got on the phone and I'll never forget her words. She said, 'Listen boys. I'm going to tell you three things, and I don't want you to ever forget them. I don't want you. I don't love you. And I never want to see you again.' "

Eddie shook his head. "That's terrible. I can't believe anybody could be that cruel."

"Believe it, Eddie. I met their mother about a month later, and you've never seen a colder heart. She had dropped by the ranch rather unexpectedly one day to bring us some of the boys' clothes. For a moment, I prayed that she had had a change of heart, but I can only guess now that she was cleaning out the last memories of her two sons.

"Unfortunately, Chris and Jimmy spotted her car just as she was pulling away. They went berserk. One of them grabbed the door handle and started screaming, 'Mommy! Mommy! Come back!' But she just looked straight ahead and pushed down on the accelerator.

Then, the other boy — I can't remember which — runs up and grabs onto the back bumper of her car as she started driving away. Eddie, I'm not exaggerating. She dragged that boy at least fifty yards before he finally let go of the bumper.

"He lay there so still in the road for what must have been a full sixty seconds before I finally caught up to him. I was scared she had knocked him unconscious or broken a bone. But he was all right — at least physically. Poor guy. His head was dug down in that gravel road and he was just lying there, crying his eyes out. I think he had finally given up."

The room fell silent, and no one said a word for several seconds as the image hung in their minds. John stood up from the table and started to clear the plates. Then he turned to look at his dinner guest, who was staring at the floor.

"Eddie, as beautiful as this ranch is, it's filled with some of the most tragic young lives that you can imagine. I believe God has provided Big Oak as a resting place to heal some of these broken hearts. Our biggest frustration, though, is that for every boy here at the ranch, there are countless more of them out there. We just have to do the best we can in our small corner of the world to lend a hand to the boys that God leads to us."

"John," Eddie said, "I want to help."

"We'll get started first thing in the morning. Now why don't you head on back to the Hilton and get a good night's sleep."

Eddie stood up from the table, picking up his plate and silverware.

"No, Eddie," Tee protested. "John and I'll get the dishes. You've had a long day. Go get some rest."

"Well, thanks, guys. The steak was great!" Eddie said, patting his stomach.

"You're very welcome," John said. "Now get outta here."

Eddie smiled, his eyes beginning to droop a little with sleep. "Well, thanks again." He turned and headed toward the front door. Before he stepped outside, he heard John call out his name in a low voice. Eddie stopped and looked back over his shoulder.

"Eddie, God's going to bless your days here at the ranch. ... Get a good night's sleep."

✣ ✣ ✣

Lying on his back and on top of the sheets of his bed, Eddie stared into the deep-dark black of his room and listened to the night sounds outside. Despite his exhaustion and a full stomach, his mind still whirled with the stories he had heard over dinner. He prayed that God would show him the way to help some of the boys at Big Oak.

"God, this is so overwhelming," he prayed. "I hardly know where to begin. Please ..."

Eddie froze. Something had brushed by his right leg. Something alive. He waited a few seconds, then started to wonder if he had imagined it. The room was too dark to see.

"Hey!" Eddie yelled out as he felt the movement again.

He switched on the lamp beside his bed just in time to see a tiny brown field mouse run across his stomach. Eddie jumped and stood straight up in the bed, kicking frantically at his unwelcome visitor. The mouse scurried down the side of the bed frame and across the floor before disappearing into one of the cabin's many open cracks.

His heart still racing, Eddie sat back down on the bed. He was embarrassed by his reaction to a harmless mouse and hoped that John and Tee had not heard his yelling. He lay back, then swung the top half of his body down toward the floor to investigate under his bed. There was nothing.

Sighing a breath of relief, he switched off his lamp and closed his eyes. He tried to pick up where he had left off in his prayers, but the interruption had befuddled his memory. Giving up, Eddie rolled over on his side and forced himself to clear his mind and concentrate on sleep. Several minutes passed, and he began to dream. He dreamed about a mouse — a big mouse. The monstrous critter was chomping away at his house, chewing and eating the rafters. The crunching noise kept growing louder and louder.

Eddie bolted out of his sleep and sat straight back up again in his bed. It was not a dream. He was really hearing something moving around somewhere in his room. Holding his breath and cocking his head, Eddie sat still and listened. He heard it again — a very distinct shuffling noise from up in his attic.

It's either a squirrel or a very big mouse, Eddie thought. Well, even if it's Big Foot, I'm too tired to look.

Again, he cut the lights, then wrapped the pillow around his head to muffle the sounds of his irritating roommates. As he finally drifted off to sleep, he could almost hear the echo of John Croyle's voice: "Welcome, Eddie, to the Big Oak Hilton."

Chapter Fourteen

The next morning, Eddie arose early despite his lack of sleep from the night before. He was excited about his first full day at the ranch, a Sunday, and looked forward to meeting the boys.

He dressed for church, then walked around the grounds for a few minutes killing time as he waited for John and Tee.

Driving over to the boys' homes with the Croyles, John asked Eddie about his first night at the Hilton. "Did you sleep well, Mr. Staub?"

"Like a baby," Eddie answered.

"No unwelcome visitors during the night?"

Eddie's face turned red, thinking John must have heard him scream when he saw the mouse.

"Well, I …"

John interrupted, laughing. "Eddie, I'm sorry. I forgot to tell you that you're sharing your humble abode with a 'possum!"

"What?"

"Didn't you hear it? It crawls around at night up in the attic. Every time we shoo it away, it always comes back home eventually.

So we've given up. Sorry about that."

"Oh yeah, well that's all right. I thought it was a squirrel or something, but it was no big deal."

"Well, good," John said. "I think you'll find the little guy is pretty harmless once you get used to all the racket. Besides, there are a lot bigger problems to tackle around here, as I'm sure you gathered from our conversation last night."

"Speak for yourself, honey," Tee retorted. "Eddie, I won't set foot in the Hilton just knowing that 'possum or some other creature might be crawling around in there."

All three were still chuckling as their van pulled up to the first boys' home. The front door of the house opened, and eight boys of various heights, shapes and ages came bounding out. Eddie immediately spotted the twins, Chris and Jimmy.

"Okay, boys," John said after getting out of the van. "I want you all to meet Eddie."

Later that morning in church and throughout the rest of the day, Eddie began a long, hot summer of breaking the ice with more than fifteen new little brothers. One by one, he worked his way through their barriers of shyness, fear, depression, and myriad other troubled emotions. The process was slow, often frustrating, but Eddie pushed on. Along the way, there were plenty of mistakes, some in dealing with the kids — but a lot more in trying to overcome his lack of experience in farming. As a sign that at least some of the kids were beginning to warm up to Eddie, one of the boys took great delight in embellishing a story about his teaching Eddie how to milk a cow.

"I told Eddie, 'That's not going to work,'" Charlie said one night at the supper table with his houseparents, who had invited Eddie over for dinner. "Then Eddie, he come back at me and said, 'Why not? I haven't even started yet!'

"Then I said, 'Well, first off, you got yourself a bull. They won't give you no milk.'"

As the table erupted in laughter, Eddie briefly thought about setting the record straight, or at least correcting Charlie's English, but let it go.

That summer, Charlie and the rest of the boys taught Eddie as much as — if not more than — he tried to teach them. By the end of the summer, Eddie had made up his mind. This was God's calling. There was so much that he wanted to accomplish at Big Oak and he didn't want to see it end after only three months.

John and Tee Croyle likewise had grown fond of Eddie. Together, they thanked God for bringing him to the ranch and prayed that he might stay on. During one of his regular evening dinners at the Croyles — they had quickly discovered Eddie's lack of talent for cooking — Eddie gave them their answer.

"Guys, if you'll have me, I'd like to continue my employment here," Eddie said in between bites at the supper table. "I've really enjoyed working with you, the houseparents — and of course the boys."

"Eddie, we feel the same way," John said. "And of course you can stay."

"We thought you'd never ask," Tee said, hugging her arms around Eddie's neck. "But what will you do about your job at Campbell High?"

"Well, I'll just have to call my principal first thing tomorrow. But before that, I've got to run this past my mother. I'm not sure she's going to be exactly happy about this."

Eddie was right. The next morning, when he called his mother at home to inform her of his decision, he received a less than enthusiastic reaction.

"Mom, I've decided to quit my job in Fairburn and continue working at Big Oak. This is hard to explain, but I really feel like this is God's purpose for me."

There were a few seconds of silence on the other end of the line before, finally, his mother spoke. "Eddie, I'm not so sure about this. Is this really the life that you want? I mean, how do you think you could support a wife and a family on the money you'll make there?"

"Mom, I just have to trust the Lord."

"Well, Eddie, all I've got to say is that if this is really God's will, then it will happen. This is a very big decision and you need to be sure. Go back to school and get your master's first. That way, if this Big Oak thing doesn't work out a few years from now, at least you'll have the credentials to get a good job somewhere."

Eddie started to protest. His desire to work at Big Oak was so strong. But his love and respect for his mother were even bigger.

"Okay, Mom. I'll think about going back to Auburn. But if I do, I'm not so sure the end result will be any different. This is something that I've prayed a lot over, and I really feel God calling me to work with a children's home."

A few days later, Eddie made his decision. He would honor his mother's wishes and return to Auburn that fall of 1980 to seek a graduate degree in physiology. Big Oak would have to wait.

Chapter Fifteen

Rodney squirmed in a hard wooden captain's chair in the vestibule outside the office of DeKalb Elementary's principal, Ann Jarret. His mother stood beside him nervously smoking a cigarette. The two waited in silence as varying tones of voices murmured behind an old and scarred wood-paneled door.

Sally Hudgins' hands trembled and she nearly dropped her cigarette while pulling a long drag of smoke into her lungs. "Rodney," she whispered harshly, "do you know how much you've hurt me? Is that why you do all these bad things? Just to hurt me?"

Rodney pretended not to hear. He twirled a pencil between his fingers.

"Stop that!" she spat, slapping her son's hands. "Put that back on the desk."

Rodney flipped the pencil across the room, sending it within a few inches of the office door in front of him. Before his mother could respond, the door opened and out walked Principal Ann Jarret, Assistant Principal Jim Reynolds, and a teacher, Gladys Earhart. The pencil snapped in two, unnoticed, under the heavy feet of Mrs. Jarret.

"Mrs. Hudgins?" asked the corpulent principal. "Would you and your son join me inside my office, please?"

Mr. Reynolds and Mrs. Earhart walked past Rodney and his mother and through a door leading to the hallway outside. The door closed behind them. Mrs. Jarret would handle the matter herself.

"Rodney, you created quite a stir around here yesterday," she said after sitting down in the cushioned seat of her office chair. "Do you want to explain yesterday's fight and then why you left the campus grounds?"

Rodney said nothing. He had not spoken a word since the police returned him home the night before. He hadn't even cried when his mother whipped him across his naked bottom and legs with a fresh-green switch she ripped from a small shrub outside their apartment's back door.

"He ain't spoken a word since last night. I'm sorry," said Rodney's mother with a mixture of anger and embarrassment in her voice.

"Mrs. Hudgins, your son's behavior of late has been very disruptive for the educational process that we are trying to conduct here at DeKalb Elementary. And this time, I'm afraid he has stepped too far across the line."

Mrs. Jarret turned toward Rodney and lowered her chin to observe him over the rim of her bifocals. "Young man, your misbehavior yesterday might have been tolerated had it been contained within the school grounds. But your leaving the campus caused a whole lot of problems for people outside our walls, primarily the county police department, which has much more important things to do than combing the streets for an irresponsible little boy."

Rodney folded his arms, stuck his chin into his chest, and stared blankly at his mud-stained tennis shoes.

"I was, and still am, of the opinion that Rodney deserves a three-day suspension," Mrs. Jarret said, firmly locking her stare on the subject of her frustration. "However, after conferring with Mr. Reynolds and Mrs. Earhart, I find my dissenting view to be in the minority."

Sally Hudgins scrunched her forehead into a dozen wrinkles. This educated talk was like listening to a foreign tongue.

The principal paused and seemed to realize her coyness was missing its mark. "I'm sorry, Mrs. Hudgins. I'll get straight to the point. We, or rather Mr. Reynolds and Mrs. Earhart, feel that a suspension would do no good for Rodney at his young age. Therefore, he will remain in school for now, though we will insist that he begin meeting with our school counselor for one hour after school every day until he straightens himself out."

"Yes ma'am. I'll make sure he goes every day. Rodney, do you understand?"

Rodney peered outside the office door at the broken pencil on the floor. He said nothing.

"Mrs. Hudgins, it's Friday and it's been a long week. Why don't you take your son home for the rest of the day and we'll hope for a fresh start on Monday."

"Yes ma'am. I think that's a real good idea. Thank you."

Rodney jumped from his seat and walked toward the door.

"You wait just a minute, Rodney!" his mother said, humiliated by her son's insolence. "I want you to thank Mrs. Jarret for giving you another chance."

Rodney continued walking out the door and into the school's main hallway. He shoved both hands inside his pants pockets, leaned against a wall and waited.

"I'm so sorry, Mrs. Jarret." Crushing out her smoking cigarette in the ashtray beside her, Sally Hudgins rose from her seat and followed her son out the door.

"I am too, Mrs. Hudgins."

✝ ✝ ✝

Sally Hudgins lighted up her third cigarette of the hour before starting her car and backing out of the school visitors' parking lot. Beside her on the front seat, Rodney pressed his nose against the car window and stared at nothing. With his face turned, Rodney's mother couldn't see the tears beginning to stream down her son's cheeks.

"Rodney, why do you hurt me so? Do you really hate me that bad?"

His mother's words pierced him like a knife, but Rodney continued his stubborn silence. His mouth quivered as he fought desperately to keep from sobbing out loud. Pent-up emotion rammed hard at barriers throughout every inch of his body, finding its only release through the tiny corner ducts of his eyes. His tears grew larger in size and fell one by one onto a knee of his blue jeans until a small, dark wet spot formed.

His mother leaned forward in her seat and pressed down on the car's accelerator as she pulled around a blue, rusty 1962 Ford pickup parked across from the school entrance. Rodney stared inside the truck at a man whose profile seemed vaguely familiar. But his watery vision was too blurred to focus.

A few seconds later, the engine of the old pickup groaned, then turned over reluctantly. The pistons fired and the truck lurched forward. Inside, Sergeant Jack Hudgins smiled. He couldn't help thinking how much Rodney had grown since he had last seen him. In fact, he doubted he would even have recognized the boy as his own flesh and blood had he not been with his mother. Lucky for me, he thought, that Sally still looks the same.

The truck's engine backfired loudly, then skipped for a second before finding the proper gear. Slowly, it pulled away from the curb and rattled down the street in sly pursuit.

Chapter Sixteen

"Couldn't you just be like everybody else?"

His mother's words still bounced around in Eddie's head as he unpacked his suitcase and settled back into the Big Oak Hilton for the second time. The past twelve months during 1980 and 1981 had been a nice break, despite the long hours of studying physiology, anatomy and other courses related to his master's. Eddie had put forth a much better effort toward his books this time around. He had actually enjoyed the studying as he savored what likely would be his last stint as an Auburn University student.

Still, his desire to return to Big Oak never wavered — which greatly concerned Teleete Staub. In her heart, she had always felt that her oldest son's nonmaterialistic nature was God's way of preparing him for the priesthood someday. Now she was confused. Eddie wanted to throw away his education for a minimum-wage job helping underprivileged kids. She particularly worried about his sparse living arrangements. But she also knew her son well enough to know there was no changing his mind. He would have to see this experiment through for himself. She just hoped his choice would not come back to hurt him or his future family if it all turned out to be a mistake.

Eddie was hired as Big Oak's assistant director in September 1981. Picking up where he had left off a year earlier, he dove happily into his new position and quickly gained more responsibilities. He soon learned there was a lot more to operating a children's ranch than working with children. There were constant staff meetings and always a long list of daily physical-plant repairs. Perhaps most important among the ranch's peripheral functions, however, was fundraising — a job that the charismatic John Croyle handled masterfully. Watching and working under John's example, Eddie began to discover and nurture his own hidden talent for public speaking and motivating large audiences of potential donors. It was a gift that would come in handy down the road, though he could hardly begin to imagine how.

Running a boys' ranch — especially one in its formative stages — was not without its problems. As Eddie became closer friends with his boss, he began to see that even John Croyle and his usually unflappable nature were not immune to the job's pressures. The first summer after Eddie's return, during preparations for an open house gathering for the Gadsden community, an electrical short wiped out all power to the outlets at the Big Oak pavilion where a large crowd was invited for supper. With only an hour to go before the big event, John had exploded in anger and red-faced frustration. It was a rare display, but Eddie realized there must have been countless other times that his friend had borne Big Oak's pressures secretly within himself. In fact, Eddie himself surely had caused John to experience more than a few "short circuits" beneath his calm veneer, Eddie figured. For although he cared deeply for the boys at Big Oak, Eddie often was unsure of the best way to show it. During his first months back at the ranch, Eddie tended to be too authoritarian. Several times, John had to pull Eddie aside and ask that he learn to loosen his reins. Slowly, Eddie began to adjust to his new environment as he discovered that working with each boy at his own individual level often was the best approach. "To nurture, not punish" became Eddie's private motto.

✝ ✝ ✝

"Eddie, several of our boys took off again last night. Could you lead a posse for us?" asked Gary Evans, one of Big Oak's houseparents, during one especially cold morning in November 1981.

Eddie stood up from his desk where he had been working since daybreak. He often was the first in and last out at Big Oak's administrative office. "Pretty cold morning to be a runaway, isn't it?" Eddie said.

"Yeah, I thought they'd all be back by now. But only two have come home for a hot breakfast. The rest are still out there making their break over the wall."

Eddie smiled and shook his head. Runaways at Big Oak were fairly commonplace.

"Got any idea where they're headed?"

"Well, as usual, Mickey seems to be the ringleader, and one of our kids mentioned a few days ago that the little guy's been talking a lot lately about leading the life of a hobo on a train."

"Okay," Eddie said. "Guess I'll start hiking the railroad tracks then."

"Thanks, Eddie. If you haven't found them by noon, I'll give you a hand. But I've got some business in town this morning."

"No problem, Gary."

Eddie pulled on a gray hooded Auburn jacket and began walking toward a nearby stretch of rail that passed to the west of the ranch grounds. Thirty minutes and a mile later, he spotted an abandoned boxcar parked on the tracks in a deserted wooded area.

"Looks like a hobo spot to me," Eddie said to himself as he began jogging — more from a need to warm himself than to hurry — toward the boxcar. His hunch was right. Inside, he found Mickey preparing a breakfast of crackers and cheese. Nearby, a cigarette was burning on a makeshift ashtray, a sawed-off two-by-four.

"Mickey, where's the rest of your gang?"

"They done left. Got too cold for 'em," Mickey answered through a mouthful of mushy crackers.

"And what do you plan to do? You know you're supposed to be in school today."

"I don't care."

"Mickey, where are you running to?"

The fourteen-year-old boy's face, already red from the cold, appeared to blush even darker. He said nothing.

"Mickey, what's the point of running away? You know that Big Oak is all you have."

Eddie later regretted his words. They spelled the truth, but he hadn't meant for them to sound as cold as the temperature that frosted his breath that day inside the old rusty rail car.

Mickey stood up, extinguished the cigarette with the sole of his shoe, then jumped from the car, nearly losing his balance as his feet hit the hard ground below. Without another word between them, the pair walked together back to Mickey's "home away from no home." For both of them, it was just another day at Big Oak Ranch.

✢ ✢ ✢

During the ensuing winter at Big Oak, Eddie developed such close ties with John and Tee, ranch secretary Diane Chavers, and the kids and houseparents, that he felt as if he had been adopted into one big family. One person in particular, a social worker named Eleanor Cox, became the sister Eddie never had. Eleanor had graduated from Mountain Brook High School three years after Eddie and later attended the University of Alabama-Birmingham, where she received her undergraduate degree in social work along with a post-graduate degree.

In addition to growing up in the same hometown, Eddie and Eleanor also shared the stigma of "wasting" a college degree on a low-paying job. Also like Eddie, Eleanor was not interested in making money for the sake of making money. Her upbeat, spunky personality was evidence that she simply loved working with children and bringing sunshine into their lives. Although Eddie was just as close, if not closer, to John Croyle, there were some things he could only share with Eleanor — like his growing restlessness at Big Oak.

"Eleanor, after six months at Big Oak, I'm not so sure anymore that this is what God has planned for my life," Eddie said.

He and Eleanor had been working several late nights that week in the administration building, finishing a stack of reports for Alabama's Department of Family and Children Services. Both were exhausted, and Eddie always seemed to confess his soul late at night. Darkness and an unwound body clock never failed to lull his normally well-guarded defenses.

"Eddie, don't say that! You love working with kids!"

"I don't mean that exactly. You're right — I do feel a calling to work with needy children. But I'm not so sure it's here at Big Oak."

"Do you feel like you'll always be in John's shadow?" Eleanor, as usual, was incredibly perceptive about Eddie's feelings. They had become that close.

"Yeah, I really hadn't thought of it exactly that way, but I think that's part of it. I guess I'm feeling something — maybe God — tugging at me to start a boys' ranch of my own."

Eddie paused, glancing at Eleanor to gauge her reaction.

"Does that sound like I'm not loyal to Big Oak?" Eddie asked. "Because it's not that way at all. John is about as close to being my brother as either Bobby or Billy."

"Oh … no, no, Eddie. I think I know exactly how you feel. But you shouldn't feel guilty. I mean, you and John are so much alike in many ways, and one of those ways is that you're both natural leaders."

"Thanks."

"Well, it's true. And I'd bet that John would feel the same way if the roles were reversed."

"Sometimes, it's hard to know what God wants me to do. I was so sure just six months ago that Big Oak was my calling, but now I feel like I was only half-right."

"Maybe God has been using Big Oak to prepare you. It could be a training ground for something else, … maybe not even a boys' ranch but another type of ministry."

"No," Eddie said, looking straight into Eleanor's dark brown eyes. "These past few months, if nothing else, have convinced me that I have a strong burden for children who are hurting. That's one thing I'm really certain about — I believe God wants me to use my gifts to help children who don't have the same opportunities that we had growing up."

"Then I think you ought to talk to John. I'm sure he'd understand. He might even suggest something that you haven't thought of."

"Not yet. I've got a little more thinking to do."

"I'm so tired, Eddie, I don't want to even think about doing any more thinking."

They both laughed in the easy spontaneous manner that long, late nights always seemed to elicit.

"We'll talk some more about this later — that is, if you want to talk to me about it," Eleanor said as she stood to leave.

"Yes, I do, Eleanor. Thank you. You're a good friend."

"You are, too. Sweet dreams."

"Same to you. Good night."

✢ ✢ ✢

Eddie's late-night confession put into words what he had been hiding in the back of his mind for several weeks. Even he was surprised by the strength of his convictions when they finally were unlocked and released out loud to Eleanor.

The next afternoon, she strolled into his office carrying a Bible. She placed the black leather-bound book, her own, on top of a stack of reports covering Eddie's desk. It was opened to the 29th chapter of Jeremiah. Eddie looked up with eyes that questioned.

"Eddie, I believe that God has impressed upon me to share this with you. Read verses five through seven." She stepped back, closed the door of his office, and waited by his side as Eddie studied the brief passage.

> "Build houses and live in them; and
> plant gardens, and eat their produce.

Take wives and become the fathers of
sons and give your daughters to hus-
bands that they may bear sons and
daughters; and multiply there and do
not decrease. And seek the welfare of
the city where I have sent you into
exile, and pray to the Lord on its behalf; for in its welfare you will have
welfare."

Eddie recognized the reading. In fact, he had read the words a
few nights earlier in his bed. Nevertheless, he reread the verses before looking back into Eleanor's smiling face.

"Eddie, I believe that you can do it. And I believe that you need
to leave."

Eleanor's confidence was reassuring. During the next several
days, Eddie could hardly go a minute without slipping into day-
dreams of starting his own boys' ranch. Privately, he began to build
his own vision, assembling the strong points of Big Oak together
with those of other ranches that he had visited as part of his job. As
this picture focused more clearly inside his head, Eddie became more
certain that he must leave Big Oak.

On a number of occasions, Eddie had discussed the ranch's future direction with John, whose ambition was to shelter as many
children as possible; he had set a goal of 100. Eddie, on the other
hand, wanted fewer children and bigger homes. During his travels
to other children's homes with eighty or more kids, Eddie would
ask the counselors what they would do differently if they could
start over. The answer almost always came back the same: fewer
kids. Eddie believed that after a campus grew past fifty young residents, it risked compromising a home-like atmosphere so critical to
a child's development. If anything should be bigger, Eddie thought,
it should be the children's living space. Why should these boys deserve any less than a traditional two-story home like the one he
grew up in?

If all of this were ever to come about, Eddie knew it would require money — a lot of money. He had seen many fine children's

homes that struggled financially to meet daily operational costs in addition to debt payments on ambitious building programs. The thought of coming up with the necessary funding was more than a little daunting, something that Eddie preferred not to dwell on. He remembered the wise words several years earlier from a close friend of the family, a Catholic nun. "Faith," she used to say, "is having one foot on the ground, one foot in the air, and a sick feeling in your stomach." Eddie now knew firsthand what she was really talking about.

The location of Eddie's ranch was another critical question that he had to answer. First and foremost, the area had to have a real need for a children's home. Second, it must be near a strong business center where necessary financial resources could be tapped. He also would want access to a quality school system and medical community.

With these parameters in mind, Eddie pointed his search toward the Alabama coastal city of Mobile, where his father's parents had lived for many years. It was far enough away to avoid overlapping Big Oak's service area yet still within the familiar surroundings of his home state. Although the city met Eddie's list of criteria, he learned from child-care advocates there of a similar effort already underway to establish a children's home. Not wanting to split the community, Eddie backed off and pointed his compass toward Chattanooga, Tennessee. Again, he found a similar situation: Another group already had expressed plans to start a children's home in the area. His random search finally swung around to Atlanta, Georgia, about a three-hour drive to the east on Interstate 20.

Surprisingly, Eddie discovered that the burgeoning population bases northeast of Atlanta had only two tiny facilities housing up to sixteen underprivileged boys. They were woefully insufficient for a state that had recorded more than 22,000 reports of child abuse and neglect in 1981. The critical need was verified emphatically in Eddie's phone-call discussions with various officials from the state Department of Family and Children Services in several Northeast Georgia counties as well as with representatives of numerous child advocacy groups.

Eddie's excitement began to spark. Finally, his dreams seemed to be taking on a real mission. By the spring of 1982, nine months after leaving Auburn and returning to Big Oak, he was convinced more than ever that it was time to depart. Mixed with his enthusiasm, however, was an intense feeling of sadness and dread. Eddie knew he could no longer put off his good friend John. He would have to tell him. And it would be one of the hardest things he had ever done.

Since his late-night talks with Eleanor several weeks earlier, Eddie had encountered numerous opportunities to confide in John. Eddie, John and Tee still ate dinner together nearly every evening in the couple's home. There also were several car rides together running errands, one-on-one office meetings, and private prayer sessions. Eddie bypassed chance after chance until he could stand it no longer. A few days into May, on a warm spring evening, he and John were walking together to one of the children's homes for a get-together. It was then that Eddie finally mustered a flash of courage. Like ripping off an old and way overdue Band-Aid, Eddie dove headlong into a silent pause between them, blurting out his secret.

"John, I think the Lord is calling me to start a children's home."

The quiet of the surrounding night returned and John said nothing. He breathed in, slowly tucked both hands into the pockets of his Levi's, and continued walking in silence. In the darkness, Eddie could not see the weight of betrayal that this friend, this man whom he loved like a brother, must have felt bearing down across his shoulders.

Eddie's heart pounded in his chest, so loud that he wondered if John could hear it. Finally, John spoke.

"What are you going to call it?"

"Eagle Ranch."

John exhibited no response, though his walk seemed to slow a bit as they approached the first boys' home along the road.

Attempting to fill the silence, Eddie interjected with an explanation. "I took the name from one of my favorite Bible verses as a kid. The one from Isaiah that says 'they shall mount up with the wings of an eagle.'" He hoped John — or anyone else — would never think that the idea had been borrowed from Eddie's alma mater mascot, the Auburn War Eagle.

"I see," John said.

Together, they stopped at the front stoop of the home of houseparents Gary and Carolyn Evans. Before they could knock, Gary opened the door to greet them, and Eddie knew there would be no more discussion — at least for the time being — of Eagle Ranch.

"Come on in, guys," Gary said, waving his hand inside.

"Thanks," said John in an upbeat voice that masked any hint of the news he had just learned. "I think I smell something cooking!"

"Carolyn may have a little surprise in the oven for us later on," Gary said. He rubbed his stomach and laughed.

Doubt it beats my own surprise, Eddie thought a little sadly to himself.

That evening, John and Eddie led a Bible devotional as they had many times before during their past eight months together. Neither let on to the turmoil swirling inside. And that night, Eddie already could feel himself pulling away from John. Their friendship was one of the closest in his life, but he knew that whatever happened between them as a result of his leaving, it could not and must not interfere with his quest to start Eagle Ranch.

Though his time at Big Oak had been brief, Eddie found himself reminiscing as if it had been his entire life. The devotionals that he shared and often led at Big Oak would always be his favorite memories with the kids. With God's help, Eddie knew there would be many more memories to start somewhere in Georgia — and with other boys who needed just as much love and a helping hand.

After the devotional that night, Eddie noticed Mickey cock his head toward a back hallway as a small band of his young friends slipped away from the gathering in silent obedience. Curious, Eddie waited a minute, then headed in their direction toward a rear bedroom. The door was cracked slightly, allowing Eddie to hear the low sounds of murmuring on the other side. Carefully, he crouched to one side to avoid being seen as he listened to the whispering of an easily recognizable voice.

"Okay, guys. Is everybody with me?" Mickey, Big Oak's round-the-clock schemer, was at it again.

"Now, if we're all courageous and nobody backs out, we can take over Big Oak Ranch."

Eddie had to bite his lip to squelch a laugh. Mickey was answered by what sounded like a skeptical chorus of five or six "okays." Oh boy, Eddie thought. A huge smile was still spread across his face. Devotionals *and* Mickey — those are two of the things I think I'm going to miss most about this place.

✛ ✛ ✛

Eddie gave John and Big Oak two-months' notice, red-circling July 9, 1982, on his calendar as the day he would leave Big Oak. During much of this interim, he began the necessary preparations for his journey to Georgia. Letters of recommendation were collected from John Croyle, the principal of Campbell High and other former employers. Knowing virtually no one in the entire state of Georgia, Eddie knew he would need some sort of credentials before calling on potential contributors and organizers. He also collected letters from juvenile authorities in the north Georgia area that confirmed the need for a place like Eagle Ranch.

There was no turning back now, but Eddie was bolstered with the encouragement imparted by the Big Oak staff and, surprisingly, from his brother Billy, usually the most pragmatic of the Staub brothers. Billy's confidence and excitement about the Eagle Ranch plan solidified Eddie's resolve. His mother, as he expected, still worried. Nevertheless, even Teleete Staub had begun to acquiesce, realizing Eagle Ranch must be more than a passing fancy if the flame of her son's passion still burned so brightly after two years of school and minimum wages. "Eddie, I know you want this," she had said. "So I'm just going to worry a lot. And I guess I'll pray a lot more, too."

With his mother's help, Eddie had secured a place to stay at a Catholic retreat off Riverside Drive in north Atlanta. The Ignatius House was operated by several Jesuit priests who had studied with his father during Ed Staub's early Jesuit training. Father John Schroder, one of his father's closest friends there, had enthusiastically offered temporary residence to Eddie upon learning that he was "Brother's son." The rent was free — a welcome blessing on a budget of thirty to forty dollars a week. Eddie had accumulated a small savings from his teaching job in addition to some money from his grandfather. He knew it would not last long, but he promised himself not to ask his mother for any portion of her fixed income. Besides, any request for money would only make her worry more. No, Eddie had told himself, I'll just have to rely on faith. And somehow, I'll get by.

July 9 came faster than Eddie thought it would, but by the time it came, he was ready. John was ready, too, for he seemed to have drifted further and further away from Eddie during the past sixty days. Eddie certainly knew Big Oak would do fine without him, but he had begun to realize that his friendship with John might not fare quite as well. Of course, they would always remain friends, but he doubted they would ever recapture the closeness of their first and second years together. The realization hurt Eddie deeply, but, like John, he already had pulled away as his heart became more attuned to the vision of Eagle Ranch. He prayed to God that John would understand. But most of all, he prayed that he was doing God's will.

Chapter Seventeen

Sally Hudgins watched her son from the corner of her right eye, driving with the other focused on the road ahead. Throughout their trip home, Rodney had continued to stare out the car window, saying nothing. She flipped her blinker to signal a left turn and steered the car through the entrance of the Rockbridge Apartments and into the first available parking space. Before she could push the gearshift into "park," Rodney sprang back to life, bolting from the car to the front door of their small apartment home. Lifting up a weathered, clay flower pot near the doorstep, he retrieved a key and shoved it roughly back and forth into the door handle until it opened.

"Rodney!" she cried, leaping from the car and following him inside. "I want you to head straight to your room. No television. You hear me?"

There was no answer.

The loud bang of a screen door clapped from across the room in the adjoining kitchen. Sally knew immediately that Rodney had run out the back door and into the apartments' wooded backyard. Too tired and frustrated to follow, she collapsed onto the living room sofa and closed her eyes. This child is going to give me a nervous breakdown, she thought. He's driving me crazy.

Wearily, she forced herself to sleep, shutting out the troubled world that wobbled around her. From the apartment above, the sounds of Sally's heavy-footed neighbor marched back and forth. Two doors down in 4-A, a dog that wasn't supposed to be there barked with an annoying, high-pitched yipping sound. But Sally heard none of it, not even the truck with the defective muffler cruising through the parking lot outside her door.

✦ ✦ ✦

Rodney sprinted through the woods behind his small apartment as fast as his spindly legs would take him. After several minutes, his lungs began to ache from exhaustion. His arms and face were red with tiny-lined blood scratches from whipping thickets of briars and seedling branches in the path of his wayward trek. Finally, he ran out of gas, swaying backward momentarily as his tired body struggled to stand, then falling forward onto both knees, forming two small craters in the soft ground beneath. Everything that he had held in for the last day-and-a-half suddenly spewed out at once and Rodney began to cry in huge, gut-wrenching sobs.

Drained of what felt like his last ounce of energy, he lay on the ground and curled into a fetal position near a dead and rotting oak tree. Rodney hurt all over, but his pain was more of heart than body.

"Why!" he wanted to scream out loud, but he whispered just in case anyone was nearby. "Why do I hurt Mama so much?"

Deep down, Rodney knew his mother was the only person who even came close to ever loving him. She wasn't perfect, but she was his life. And deep down, he knew he loved her.

Beginning to feel the damp ground soaking through his jeans, Rodney forced himself to stand up. He raised the backhand sleeve of his dirty sweatshirt to his face to wipe away the mucus and tears. The effort left a dirty streak across his cheeks. Clearing his head, he assessed his latest actions and concluded that running away wouldn't solve anything — especially when there was nowhere to go. He would return home, he figured, say he was sorry and try to do better. It was all he could think of to do.

He brushed off the leaves clinging to his sweatshirt and rubbed as much of the red clay as he could from his knees. Then, having calmed himself, he turned back toward home. The hike took nearly half an hour, much longer than expected, and by the time he reached the back door of his apartment, dusk was settling in. Not one light was on inside his home. Mama must have gone to sleep, he figured.

Rodney turned the door knob halfway, then stopped. In the far corner of the parking lot, he saw an old blue truck — just like the one he had noticed that afternoon upon leaving the principal's office. He paused a few seconds in curiosity, then reached back again to open the back door. It swung out by itself, and a large man stepped out of the shadows, filling the frame.

Rodney's initial reaction was embarrassment. He instantly assumed he had opened a neighbor's back door by mistake. But before he could say "sorry," the dark figure clamped Rodney's right arm into a vise-like grip. From inside the apartment, Rodney heard his mother scream hysterically.

"Run, Rodney! Run! Run! Run!"

Before Rodney could react, the burly arm that held him jerked him violently inside. The door slammed shut behind him. From overhead, an uncovered sixty-watt light bulb switched on, briefly flickering before spreading its dim light across the room. Rodney's eyes adjusted to the gloom and immediately focused on his mother's purple, beaten face a few feet away. She was holding a pillow to her chest and trembling all over.

"Now, then," said the big man, grinning like a toothy jackal. His smooth-as-velvet voice was at odds with the panic around him. "We're all one big happy family again."

III

ALONE IN GEORGIA

Chapter Eighteen

Summer 1982

A single, salty drop of sweat hung in agonizing suspension at the end of the husky linebacker's nose. He ignored it. A much bigger annoyance was crouched directly in front of him in the form of an equally imposing six-foot, 250-pound tackle. Their two helmets came close to touching as each man hunkered into position. To one side an older man, who looked like a Marine drill sergeant, bent his knees into a half-squat. A silver whistle hung from a dirty shoestring around his clean-shaven neck. He popped it into his mouth and puffed out a blast of wind.

The soprano shrill was followed immediately by a duo of baritone grunts and the sound of several hundred pounds of colliding bone and muscle. The two men — nearly surrounded in a tightening semicircle of their teammates — bucked once, twice, and a third time before locking together into a twisting, struggling stalemate. The "sergeant" blew his whistle again, halfheartedly signaling an end to the drill, but the fight continued. Several helmets waved in the air along with shouts of encouragement. The assistant coach smiled. He liked their spirit. Only a few weeks remained before the University of Georgia's first football game of the 1982 season. It was prime time to pump up the intensity and enthusiasm of his troops.

On the opposite end of the practice field, far from the center of the hot August fury, stood Eddie Staub. So strange, he thought, to see the private confines of this team that had been such longtime rivals of his own alma mater. Georgia-Auburn football games, historically scheduled near the close of each season, always seemed to determine an S.E.C. championship or a post-season bowl match-up. But football and big games hardly ranked on Eddie's list of primary concerns on this Tuesday afternoon. He was there on a different mission. Vince Dooley, a standout Auburn quarterback in the 1950s and now head football coach of the Georgia Bulldogs, had agreed to lend his ear to Eddie's cause. It was Eddie's first solid break in several weeks of politely shut doors and piles of unreturned phone messages.

Vince Dooley was big … really big. The association of such a prominent and beloved sports figure with Eagle Ranch surely would open doors, Eddie believed. He already had witnessed the tremendous motivational value of football coaches Paul "Bear" Bryant of the University of Alabama and Pat Dye of Auburn in their involvement with Big Oak Ranch.

Only a few days earlier, August 4, Eddie had contacted Dooley's office from the upstairs phone of Ignatius House, the Catholic retreat where Eddie had been based for the past month. Like the majority of his cold calls, this one had ended in the same familiar "Send us some information and we'll get back to you." It was getting old, but Eddie had obliged, typing and mailing a simple, one-page letter on Ignatius House stationery. Amazingly, his effort touched off a phone call three days later from Theresa Coleman, Dooley's personal secretary. The appointment had been set for a Tuesday, August 17, during preseason summer football practice. Dooley was especially busy this time of year, but his secretary said he'd allow five minutes.

Eddie had hardly slept during the few days leading up to the meeting. Only now, standing awkwardly by himself on the well-worn artificial turf, he wondered if perhaps he had built it up too much. Did he really think it was possible for Dooley to help a stranger after one brief meeting? His throat was dry and his heart raced as he pondered what to do next.

"Hey, you!"

Eddie turned to see a short, wrinkled old man in a Bulldog-red golf shirt and khaki shorts waving his arms and running toward him. He was "Squab" Jones, a quasi-coach revered as nothing less than an institution in the halls of University of Georgia football. Considered one of Dooley's most loyal assistants, Squab watched over the coach and his practices like a hawk.

"Don't you know this is a closed practice?" Squab said, planting both hands defiantly on his hips. His raspy voice sounded out of breath. "You better have a real good reason for being here, son."

"Mrs. Coleman sent me out here," Eddie responded shakily. He already was nervous and this guy only made it worse. "I've got a meeting with Coach Dooley."

Squab paused to stare up and down Eddie's long frame. With both hands, he screwed his floppy billed UGA hat down tighter over his nearly bald head.

"He didn't say anything about a meeting to me," Squab said, still suspicious. "You better wait here while I call Mrs. Coleman myself."

He left Eddie alone to wonder whether his hour's drive to Athens had been a wasted trip. "I should have known this was too good to be true," Eddie thought.

A few minutes later, Squab waddled back onto the field, shaking his head and muttering under his breath. "Okay, you have an appointment with Coach Dooley. C'mon." Squab still wasn't happy — or convinced.

Dooley, dressed identically to Squab and the various coaches on the practice field, stood with folded arms on the faded hash mark of the fifty-yard line. Each of his assistant coaches oversaw specific player roles such as quarterbacks, offensive linemen, and running backs. Dooley watched the separate regimens, privately assessing each one in deep concentration.

"Coach, my name's Eddie Staub."

The interruption caused Dooley's brow to wrinkle momentarily before relaxing back to its original smoothness. The name did not immediately register. After a brief glance at Eddie, then at Squab, he returned his heavy gaze to the field without a word.

"Mrs. Coleman sent him out here, Coach," Squab said, absolving himself from blame. "If you want, I'll …"

"What can I do for you, Eddie?" the head coach interrupted. A tight smile was pursed on the lips of his stone face.

"Coach Dooley, I appreciate your meeting with me. Mrs. Coleman said I have five minutes of your time, so I'll be brief."

Eddie knew he better be direct. He might not have even sixty seconds. "I'm from Alabama and I came here in July to start a home for needy kids. I used to work at Big Oak Ranch near Gadsden, and Coach Bryant and Coach Dye were real involved in that program. I'd like for you to consider getting involved with this. There's a real need, especially in this area, but I can't do it by myself."

Dooley nodded politely. He undoubtedly had heard hundreds of charities plead their cases before — and probably much more polished, too, Eddie thought. He took a deep breath.

"Coach, I know you're busy, but I just want to tell you three more things and I'll let you go. I'm twenty-seven years old and all I have is a dream to give little boys a home. Number one, I don't have any money. Two, I don't have any land. And three, I don't know anyone in Georgia…" Eddie's voice caught briefly in his throat. His eyes searched desperately for Dooley's and finally connected. It was now or never.

"I'm asking you to stick your neck out for me."

Dooley glanced at Eddie, then returned his attention to the practice field. He said nothing for what seemed an eternity. Standing out of earshot a few yards away, Squab checked his watch impatiently and shook his head. The clamor on the field beckoned and begged Dooley to return. But for some reason he hung back.

"Let me make sure I heard you right," Dooley said, his arms still folded as he cocked his head slightly and studied Eddie's face. "You want to start a boys' ranch, but you don't have any land."

"No sir."

"And you don't have any money either."

"No sir."

"And you don't have *any* friends?"

"No sir, … unless you're interested."

Dooley chuckled. "It sounds like you have your work cut out for you. … What exactly do you want from me?"

"Be on my board of advisers. Make a few phone calls and open doors for me."

Dooley paused, as if to reflect. The seriousness had returned to his face. Finally, he extended his right hand. "It's Eddie, right?"

"Yes, sir." They shook hands.

"Eddie, anything you need, you just let me know."

Eddie smiled back sheepishly. He'd just made his first friend in Georgia.

✛ ✛ ✛

The Dooley meeting provided inspiration and confirmation when Eddie needed them most. His days at Ignatius House had become increasingly defeating and lonely. More than once, during numerous trips on the road meeting with potential donors and searching for land sites, he pulled his car through a drive-in automatic teller machine just to see his name spelled out in lights on the black video screen. Somehow, the white electronic words "Hello, Eddie Staub" elicited a friendly feeling that had been difficult to find in such a big city so far from Mountain Brook, Auburn, and the familiar faces of home.

It was a time that also found Eddie grappling with his purpose in giving up so much on such a long-shot dream. What was he really doing here? Would he wake up one day and realize that he had thrown away part of his life? With so much time alone, Eddie spent many hours of self-examination through prayer. Never in his life had he talked so much to God. One of his favorite places of prayer was the simple chapel within the spartan, red-brick Ignatius House. The positive reassurance from his soul-searching efforts there, boosted tremendously by Coach Dooley's surprising support, convinced Eddie to keep moving forward.

Much of that moving was done in his car, a brown 1978 Toyota Corona that looked small in comparison to Eddie's long frame. He was logging hundreds of miles every week looking for potential tracts of land for the ranch in counties he had never heard of. If necessary, he would tour every dusty back road between Atlanta and the Carolinas, weaving through small towns and farms in places with country-sounding names like Pickens, Bartow, Forsyth, and Lumpkin. He was attracted to these areas because he felt the best site for the ranch would be within a quiet, rural area north of Atlanta where he had documented the greatest need for a children's home. At the same time, he needed an area wealthy enough to support the ranch with future operational money. He also sought a balance between land that was secluded but close enough to quality schools and medical care. Finding the perfect spot, Eddie soon discovered, would not come easily.

But at least he was gaining a little more respect now. Coach Dooley had seen to that. Two weeks after their meeting, Eddie received an audience with the state's other college football kingpin, Bill Curry, head coach at Georgia Tech. Armed with their backing, Eddie promptly named both coaches as Eagle Ranch's first two advisory board members.

Meetings with other influential Georgians soon followed, including Rankin Smith, owner of the Atlanta Falcons professional football team; Truett Cathy, CEO of the Chick-fil-A restaurant chain; and A.H. Sterne, esteemed former chairman of the board at the powerful Trust Company Bank of Georgia. Their initial support was more symbolic than monetary, and more than a few doubts were expressed as to whether Eddie could pull off his quest. Still, he was encouraged. It sure beat no-show appointments and telephone hang-ups.

Eddie possessed an humbling, innocent charm that endeared

him to those who agreed to listen. Though he was always careful to present a professional image in coat and tie, his wrinkled shirt and trousers nearly always gave him away. For one appointment, he showed up at the wrong office building in downtown Atlanta; only after hailing a passing courier-service truck did he make it to the right place with seconds to spare. Another call ended in his backing into a telephone pole with his car. But such youthful innocence and awkwardness, combined with boyish good looks, were irresistible. Eddie Staub had nothing to show, no tangible proof that his vision could happen. But this was no slick salesman. Even his toughest skeptics were left with little doubts of Eddie's sincerity, purpose and strong faith. He believed in himself because he believed in God.

For all that was going right, however, there was still a lot more going wrong for Eddie and Eagle Ranch. He was living on a shoe-string budget of less than forty dollars a week. Survival was possible only because of the free lodging and occasional free meals at Ignatius House. But after two months, the arrangement unfortunately was about to end along with summer. Several retreats were scheduled soon at the center, and Eddie's room would be needed. So focused had he been on all the appointments, letter-writings and phone calls that Eddie had taken little time to search for new living quarters. Less than a week now remained at Ignatius House and he had nowhere to go.

Salvation came in a chance meeting with an out-of-touch friend. Eddie had met David Salyers only a year earlier while working to build support for Big Oak Ranch from the Chick-fil-A restaurant organization, where David worked in marketing. Chick-fil-A was noted for its support of Christian ministries, and David had allowed Eddie to conduct a devotional for a group of staff members there. Now in Atlanta, David — a fitness buff who loved to pump iron — was working out at the American Fitness Center in Sandy Springs where Eddie happened to visit in an all-too-seldom effort to keep in shape.

"Eddie, what are you doing in Atlanta?"

"David! How are you doing?"

"Great. Hey, I'm sorry we lost touch with each other, but I heard you had left Big Oak. What are you doing now?"

"Funny you should ask," replied Eddie, laughing. "I'm trying to start a boys' ranch like Big Oak here in Georgia, but I've got a slight problem at the moment."

"Oh yeah? What's that?"

"No place to stay. Right now, I'm living at a retreat center off Riverside Drive, but they've told me that I need to move out in three days."

"Are you looking for an apartment?"

"Well, not quite. I'm not working anywhere because I'm putting all my time into starting this ranch. So I'm on a pretty tight budget right now."

Salyers' grin suddenly vanished in concentration, his jet-black eyebrows pressing together in a V between his perpetually squinty eyes. "Wait a minute, wait a minute, Eddie. I might know of something. One of my colleagues at Chick-fil-A mentioned something the other day about needing a house sitter. He's leaving the company to start a restaurant in North Carolina, and I think he feels a little uneasy about leaving his house unoccupied for the next several months. Do you want me to check?"

"That'd be great, David. Thanks."

A week later, Eddie had found a new home — rent-free. He thanked God for the blessing but couldn't help wondering: Am I running out of miracles?

✣ ✣ ✣

In September 1982, Eddie moved to his new address in Powder Springs, Georgia, a small suburb northwest of Atlanta. His time there would be short — the owner planned to return by Christmas — but Eddie was thankful for any extension on his fragile stay in Georgia.

His reacquaintance with David Salyers had been another blessing. Through David, Eddie rapidly made several friends, helping to ease his feelings of isolation and loneliness. A weekly Bible study that regularly attracted hundreds of young people throughout the Atlanta area became a favorite oasis for Christian fellowship and spiritual strengthening. Organized by a Lockheed employee and lay minister named "Dad" Ellis, the meeting was held at a church near Eddie's new quarters. Ellis, who was in his late forties, was already bald as a cue ball. His head — as well as the weekly message by John Riley, a former placekicker for the Auburn football team — stood out among the throngs that attended the evening gatherings. Through Salyers, Ellis eventually learned about Eddie and his struggling crusade.

At first, he was skeptical. During his many years of youth ministry, Ellis had come across numerous well-meaning youths with high ambitions but not the patience and endurance to see them through. But something seemed different, Ellis figured, about Eddie Staub. In a rare departure from his usual agenda at Metro Bible Study, Ellis invited Eddie to take the floor for five minutes at a future meeting to talk about his Eagle Ranch vision. Eddie was surprised by Ellis' invitation and thrilled by this acceptance from such a well-known Christian leader.

Prior to that time, Eddie had discussed his Eagle Ranch mission mostly on a one-on-one basis. Never had he had the chance to reach so many people at one time. The night of his talk, more than 2,000 people crowded the sanctuary of Mt. Paran Church of God. Silently praying under his breath for the right words to say, Eddie stepped up to the pulpit and delivered an inspiring message of faith, clearly touching many in the crowd that night. Later, Eddie realized that his witness to so many people placed increased urgency on his resolve to succeed. Eagle Ranch was becoming more than just one man's dream, and Eddie shuddered at the thought of letting down his growing number of supporters. Even more, he feared that his personal failure might be viewed as God's. That, indeed, would be a terrible burden to carry for the rest of my life, Eddie thought.

For the moment, though, Eddie was greatly encouraged by the response to his message at Metro Bible Study. He had collected praise and instant respect within a relatively small but energetic circle of Atlantans. The validation of his mission was gratifying on a personal level, but he realized that he had not made it this far on his own. A growing number of friends and supporters had greatly helped, particularly David Salyers.

Salyers' friendship was truly a godsend. What would have happened had they not run into each other that day at the gym? Eddie searched for something to show his appreciation and finally came up with an idea. It wasn't exactly a gift and hardly worth anything. But one thing was for sure — it would be from the heart. Eddie picked a Friday night at Nick's Pizza in Atlanta as the appropriate backdrop for his presentation. It was a favorite hangout for the two bachelors.

"David, I don't think I've told you enough how grateful I am that you came along. In all honesty, I don't know what I'd be doing right now if you hadn't," Eddie said between bites of a pepperoni and mushroom-supreme pizza.

Salyers' face creased into his familiar smile. He teased back at his friend: "I don't think you've thanked me enough either, Eddie!" They both laughed for a while before Eddie fell silent, staring blankly down at his plate.

Salyers read the seriousness in his friend's face. Using his napkin, he wiped off his smile along with a red smudge of sauce from his lips. He continued chewing, waiting for whatever Eddie was about to say.

"David, coming here to Georgia, where I didn't know anyone but you and maybe a few others, has been really hard. If I hadn't run into you, I don't know what I would have done."

"I don't either," Salyers cracked, his mouth curling back to a thin smile. "That stuff you told me about sticking your bank card in the automatic teller machine just so you'd know you were still somebody — a clear sign that you were going crazy!"

Eddie looked down and chuckled. He was embarrassed. "Okay, okay. So maybe that was a little strange. But, well … it's hard to explain, all right?"

They both laughed again, not so much over the bank-card story but in an involuntary attempt to cover the slight uneasiness that often exists between one man trying to express a sentiment to another.

"David, I wonder if you would consider being on my board of directors. You've really been a great sounding board. You have given me a lot of wise counsel. And I'd like for you to stay involved in this."

"Wow! I've always wanted to get involved in something like this from the ground level. But I guess this is what you'd call the basement level!"

"Is that a yes or a no?" Eddie cocked his head, smiling as he awaited an answer.

"Of course, it's a yes. I'd be glad to, Eddie."

Eddie looked deep into the smiling eyes of his friend and saw that he meant it.

✢ ✢ ✢

Four months into his journey to Georgia, Eddie tripped over a glaring weakness in his efforts toward starting a boys' ranch. He was full of enthusiasm, grand ideals, and hard work — but he was still very much naive. This embarrassing shortcoming was uncovered quite painfully during a meeting with one of Atlanta's corporate fund-raising gatekeepers, the highly respected Victor Gregory of Trust Company Bank.

Eddie was fortunate to have even made his way through the man's door. He had pulled several strings, most of them very thin and frayed. Hank Wingate, the father of a former girlfriend at Auburn, first had introduced Eddie to the past chairman of Trust Company's board, A.H. Sterne. The connection had led to a meeting with Gregory on the eleventh floor of Trust Company's intimidating downtown tower in Five Points, the heart of Atlanta's financial district. Trust Company was one of the state's oldest and largest banks, and as vice president of community affairs, Gregory was a powerful insider in the world of corporate foundations and wealthy philanthropists.

Gregory spotted Eddie as a novice within the first few minutes of their meeting. First, the young man wore an out-of-style blue blazer and cotton tie instead of the more appropriate starched white shirt and dark suit worn by those in the know of downtown Atlanta business. Second, he learned that Eddie had made very few contacts in Georgia — and even those were far from the real movers, shakers and powerful insiders that could make dreams such as his happen. Third, Eddie touted his experience with Big Oak Ranch and Campbell High School — but a few years working with kids hardly qualified someone to start and oversee a regional children's home. And finally, despite Eddie's hard work to verify the need for Eagle Ranch, Gregory questioned his thoroughness. Had he considered the potential fallout of competing with the popular Sheriffs' Boys Home in northwest Georgia and other similar operations across the state? Eddie also was unfamiliar with some of the state's key political figures in the arena of children's issues. In short, he was in way over his head.

"Mr. Staub, I hate to be the one to burst your bubble. Your heart's certainly in the right place, but I'm afraid that this dream of yours simply is not going to happen," said the wavy-haired executive, peering over his glasses from behind a heavy oak desk.

Their meeting had lasted about thirty minutes when Gregory issued the blunt assessment. Despite the cold sound of his words, the man still cringed inside each time he had to let down another Eddie Staub. But if someone doesn't wake him up now with a little scare talk, Gregory thought, he'll have to find out the hard way. Besides, from what this Mr. Staub had told him, he's practically penniless — probably only a day or so away from living on the streets!

"Listen, Mr. Staub. Let me give you a little fatherly advice, and I don't mean this to sound patronizing. You've got a splendid idea but it needs a lot more work."

Several butterflies fluttered inside Eddie's stomach through most of the meeting as he listened to this man tear down his vision. Eddie had placed so much importance on getting his foot in the door of Victor Gregory, but he had no idea it would turn out this way. The man's brutal honesty had stunned him. More than that, it had hurt him. But as the end of his appointment came nearer, his pain had gone numb. In its place, a slow-burning anger was beginning to kindle.

"Now, Mr. Staub, here's what I suggest you do. Why not go back to Alabama where at least you know some people? I'm sure they'd take you back at this Big Oak place where you could gain more experience. Then you'd be in a better position to start this ranch of yours, okay?"

Eddie smiled weakly, nodding his head politely but saying nothing.

"Now, I'm sorry but I have another appointment shortly. Please allow me to walk you to the elevator."

Gregory rose from his chair, a signal that their meeting was over. He walked to a closet on the opposite side of his large office and retrieved his suit coat. Eddie stood and waited in silence as the sharply dressed executive adjusted the sleeves of his shirt and straightened his tie. Glancing secretly from one eye, Gregory could see Eddie's defeat in the way he hung his shoulders. Poor guy.

"Eddie, the fact is that there are a lot of established, top-qualified people who wouldn't even attempt to do what you've proposed. So I hope you won't get down on yourself."

At that moment, Eddie felt something inside him spark. And then, just as Gregory reached to open his office door, it flared.

"Mr. Gregory, I appreciate what you've told me, but I'm not going back to Alabama."

Gregory stopped. He released his grip on the door handle and slowly turned around. Something he hadn't seen to that point was burning in Eddie's stare.

"Mr. Staub, I ..."

"No, Mr. Gregory," Eddie interrupted with surprising boldness. "That may be the way *you* feel, but I *am* going to build a boys' ranch, and it's going to be *here* in Georgia. And the reason that it's going to happen is because God has led me here. This is what He wants."

The two men stood still, looking straight into each other's eyes and neither saying a word for several awkward seconds. Gregory finally broke the stalemate, unlocking his stare as he walked back to his desk to pull a file from a side drawer. He motioned to a small table and two chairs off to one side of his office.

"Okay, Mr. Staub. Why don't we sit back down."

"What about your appointment?"

"Let's just sit down, okay?" He smiled. "I'm going to give you some names."

Gregory was a seasoned pro. He could spot the con artists who came walking through his door every week asking for money. And he knew when someone lacked the necessary qualifications to back up their promises. But at that instant, he realized Eddie possessed an intangible spiritual quality about him that was magnetic. It was just a hunch, but Gregory oddly found himself believing in this fresh-faced kid.

For the next half-hour, the banker reviewed a long list of key officials in the state's child-care arena. He described other "charity brokers" like himself who understood the complicated web of community needs and available sources of funding. He also named several long shots — wealthy donors with whom Eddie could try to establish rapport.

"Now Mr. Staub, I want us to have an understanding. I've decided to help you, but I wish to remain in the shadows, so to speak. You're going to have to do all the work."

"Yes, sir. I'll follow up on this list and everything you've suggested, and I'll report back in two weeks."

Gregory smiled. He had no doubt that this Eddie Staub would be back.

✢ ✢ ✢

Working from the list of names supplied by Victor Gregory, Eddie continued his uphill climb through Atlanta's bureaucratic maze of corporate and private foundations. As much as he would have preferred to sit back, pray, and let the money come raining down from the heavens, Eddie had learned a valuable lesson from his meeting with Gregory. It would take plenty of old-fashioned elbow grease before the Eagle Ranch mission could be fully realized.

One of Eddie's most difficult sales jobs continued to stir within himself. His confidence teetered back and forth as he continually forced himself to believe in Eagle Ranch — even if he couldn't blame others for not doing the same. He still had not raised the first dollar. There wasn't even a land site for the ranch that he could show off to potential donors. About the only physical representation of Eagle Ranch was a letter of incorporation typed and notarized on two legal-sized pages. But that was as it should be, Eddie rationalized. Because when Eagle Ranch finally opens, overcoming all of these impossible obstacles, people are going to have no choice but to credit the miracle solely to God.

More and more often, Eddie had begun to view his struggle in this manner. It was a philosophy that had been further molded, then fired and glazed after he came to know an Atlanta Presbyterian minister named Randy Pope. Looking at Pope — an ironic last name for a Protestant minister — was almost like looking into a mirror. Like Eddie, Pope was an Alabama native and only four years older. And he, too, had come to Georgia several years earlier to embark upon a seemingly against-all-odds mission of faith — organizing and building a church from scratch. His hard work had resulted in the founding of Perimeter Church, one of metro-Atlanta's fastest-growing places of worship. A core membership of young metro-Atlanta worshipers inspired by Pope's energy and uplifting faith was one of its keys to success.

In Pope, Eddie found a kindred spirit. He remembered a visit to his office where, hanging behind the young minister's desk, was a sign that read, "Attempt something so great for God that it is doomed to failure unless God is truly in it." Eddie wrote down the phrase on a piece of paper and vowed to keep it with him until Eagle Ranch was built. It became his silent rallying cry. If anyone doubted that Eddie could succeed, they were right. It would be God's triumph, not Eddie's.

Chapter Nineteen

North Georgia's Hall County was named after Lyman Hall, the state's first governor and one of the Colonial signers of the Declaration of Independence. Gainesville, its county seat, claimed General Edmund Pendleton Gaines, a veteran and hero of the War of 1812, as its namesake. Both men were footnotes in early American history and therefore quite suited to the plebeian character of the community that had taken their names in tribute.

Gainesville lay sixty minutes north of Atlanta on the north end of Georgia's largest lake and at the foothills of the Blue Ridge Mountains where the Appalachian Trail begins its steep ascent along the East Coast toward Maine. For many Florida and Atlanta retirees with summer homes in the cool mountains of north Georgia, Gainesville was simply a city along the way. But its humble presence was increasingly catching the attention of Eddie Staub.

The 20,000-population city, Northeast Georgia's financial and medical center, sat squarely in the middle of an area that was seriously deficient in children's services. There were no facilities in the immediate Gainesville area to house abused or neglected boys. With the exception of temporary shelters, the closest Georgia towns with any youth facilities to speak of were at least an hour's drive away: Toccoa, Ellijay, and Monroe with eight beds each. Eddie's ambitious dream for Eagle Ranch called for five homes housing eight boys each — more than the total number of beds for youth that existed throughout the entire region.

Gainesville and Hall County seemed to possess all the characteristics that Eddie had been searching for. He vaguely remembered passing through the area on a road trip a few years earlier with the wrestling team that he had helped to coach back at Campbell High School. The vision of Eagle Ranch was hardly a passing thought then, but he recalled seeing the rural surroundings of southern Hall County from his bus window and thinking that it would make a peaceful setting for a children's home — should he ever have the desire and ambition to start one.

Gainesville cloaked its riches in a string of chicken houses that covered most of the northern half of the county. For within these rickety wood structures lay the golden egg for the town's biggest moneymaker. The poultry business was top rooster in Gainesville. On a water tower along one of the roadways into town were emblazoned the bold words: "Poultry Capital of the World." Gainesville annually hatched and processed millions of chickens for dinner tables across the world. Several decades earlier, when the community lay devastated from a deadly tornado in 1936, the poultry business led the area back to prosperity. In fact, many Gainesville residents owing their wealth to chickens would reason that poultry pioneers Jesse Jewell and others after him — as opposed to either Governor Hall or General Gaines — were the community's true heroes.

Eddie learned about one of the town's most respected modern-day poultry executives shortly after he began touring the area with local Realtors in search of land for the ranch. Loyd Strickland — a tall, elderly man who cast a long shadow in Hall County — was the owner of Crystal Farms, a large chicken-hatchery operation based in south Hall County. Strickland was a quiet but strong Christian man who had supported numerous worthwhile projects for the benefit of his community. He also had a big heart for young people and was responsible for luring a national youth-ministry program called Young Life to the area in 1968.

Not wanting to wait for a formal introduction, Eddie decided to contact Strickland one day from a pay phone at the Hall County Courthouse, where he had been researching land-tract records for a possible lead. He was taken off guard a bit when Strickland, not a secretary, answered the phone.

"This is Loyd Strickland," said a raspy, elderly voice.

"Oh, hello. This is Mr. Strickland of Crystal Farms?"

"Yes it is."

"Uh, sir, my name is Eddie Staub, and I'd like to meet with you sometime to tell you about a Christian ministry that I'm trying to start. I was hoping you might be interested."

"Depends on what it is."

"It's a boys' home, or actually a boys' ranch. I'm looking to start one in an area like this one where there's such a great need."

"Mr. Staub, what is your statement of faith?"

"My what?"

"Your statement of faith." He didn't elaborate.

"Uh, are you asking if I'm charismatic or something?"

The other end of the line began to chuckle softly. "If we're going to talk, I think you need to come and see me right away."

Eddie was slightly embarrassed but thankful for the invitation. Thirty minutes later, he sat across from Strickland's desk in a wing-back leather chair that sank into a plush, richly colored oriental rug. Eddie admired the warm furnishings of the private office as well as the window view of a small private lake. In the course of his daily meetings with the high-level Georgia executives on Victor Gregory's list, he had seen many lavishly decorated offices but few as comfortable and cozy as this one.

Strickland was generous with his time. On the spur of the moment, he had allowed a full hour and a half. Eddie's sincerity touched him. There had been many others before Eddie with their hands out, but Strickland had the feeling that this young man was genuine. Eddie ran through his well-rehearsed description of Eagle Ranch, and Strickland was mildly impressed by the young man's years at Big Oak Ranch and Campbell High School. At least he wasn't some flash in the pan with no knowledge of what he was attempting. Still, the guy sure was setting his hopes high. What he really needs is a miracle, Strickland thought.

"Eddie, I tell you what. This is a big chunk you're biting off."

Eddie hardly flinched. He had heard it all too often before.

"And economic times being the way they are right now, it's really going to be hard for you to find many people who'll have the ability to contribute to your cause — even if they have the heart for it."

Eddie refrained from asking the man if he personally possessed either one of those inclinations on behalf of the ranch. Strickland certainly had not achieved his business success by immediately saying yes to every noble cause that ever walked through his door.

"I'll give you names of some people around town. If you can get them interested, then you come back and see me."

Between Victor Gregory, Strickland and others, Eddie figured he would have quite an impressive list of Georgia's Who's Who before it was all over. He was getting a little tired of the routine — especially when so many of the names either turned him down or refused to meet — but he politely said thanks while scribbling the dictation on a sheet of paper from his notebook.

A few minutes later, they stood and shook hands. Strickland patted him on the back and wished him well. And as he closed the door behind him, Eddie already was thinking ahead to his next appointment with another potential donor on Gregory's list back in Atlanta. He had no idea of the enormity of what he had just set into motion in Hall County, Georgia.

✢ ✢ ✢

Whenever Eddie thought about quitting, his stomach turned. He had quit once before, during his baseball playing days at Auburn, and it had cost him. Back then, as now, he vowed never to give up again. Once he set his mind toward a goal, he intended to keep trying until he reached it. Subconsciously, he was driven by the ugly memory of the day his baseball career died.

Eddie had done everything by the book at Auburn. He had practiced fundamentals over and over as he should have done. He had exercised regularly to keep his throwing arm strong and catcher's legs nimble. He had disciplined himself almost beyond necessity. Despite the hard work, his coaches increasingly had seemed to look the other way. Even after receiving his hard-fought scholarship, he realized that timing and talent had more to do with a starting position on the team than did dedication and sweat.

Midway into his junior year, Eddie tired of the whole regimen — especially after the loss of his father. He continued going through the motions of practice, but with less zeal. Baseball, the love of his life, had simply lost its appeal. Oddly, Eddie began playing his best baseball during this low period. Most likely, it was because he had shed the tremendous self-imposed pressure that followed him throughout his first three years on the team. Still, his head coach hardly seemed to notice — even after Eddie had boldly visited Coach Nix's office to complain about his lack of playing time. Though Eddie saw a little action in home games, he still was not on the regular traveling squad.

As his mental attitude diminished, so went his physical condition. One day at practice, while he crouched in his catcher's stance behind the plate, a batter's foul ball ricocheted squarely off Eddie's left knee. The next day, the injured knee was swollen and he could hardly walk. Depressed and feeling that the coaches couldn't care less, Eddie finally quit. Not the team, exactly, but in his heart. The next day, he failed to show up for practice. He didn't even inform his coaches — a cardinal sin that would not go unpunished. But Eddie didn't care. He was washed up. He had finally let go.

Auburn's next opponent that week was LSU in a road game to be played in New Orleans. Eddie hadn't bothered to check the list of names of the traveling squad posted outside Coach Nix's door. If he had, he would have been shocked. If he had, he would have been on the road to Louisiana.

✣ ✣ ✣

"Randy, someone on the line for you. It's long-distance."

Randy Pope glanced up from the sermon notes spread across the desk of his private office at Perimeter Church in Atlanta. His concentration had been so deep that he had only heard his secretary's voice, not what she had said.

"I'm sorry. What did you want?"

"You have a long-distance call, sir."

He picked up the sleek, black executive-phone receiver and said hello. A warm smile quickly spread across his face as he heard the voice of one of his longtime friends and supporters.

"Randy, I understand you know a young man named Eddie Staub."

"Sure do. Great guy with a lot of faith."

"Could you tell me how to get in touch with him?"

"Sure. I've got his address and phone number right here in my Rolodex. He lives somewhere in Powder Springs. Just a second ..."

Chapter Twenty

Sally Hudgins no longer felt the pain. There was nothing but total numbness. Lifting her head in slow motion, she strained to see. She strained to listen. Nothing. Her surroundings were total black and dead silence.

She reached out into the darkness and felt nothing. Then, bringing her hand down to her side, she became aware of a hard, smooth surface below her. She was lying on a floor. How long had she been there? Slowly, she tried lifting her head. Every movement was an effort and it all seemed like a fuzzy dream.

In the corner of one eye, she caught a brief glimpse of something that glowed. Her head collapsed in exhaustion before she had time to focus. Again, she tried. Gathering up the little strength that remained in her body, she pulled her neck back until her head was completely off the floor. Above her and to the right, she saw the glowing light again. This time, she recognized it: her digital bedroom clock. The tiny bit of information registered in her brain, and she slowly regained her bearings. She was on the floor of her bedroom.

"Rodney!" she cried out. There was no answer.

Then she remembered.

Panicked, she felt a surge of adrenaline rush through her body and she struggled to sit up. All at once, the pain returned. Her head throbbed, and a loud buzz filled her ears. Her body screamed in protest, and she felt her brain ordering her to slip back under the cover of unconsciousness. She began letting go until, once again, she remembered.

Terror took over, and she forced her way through the pain to stay awake. The clock came back into focus. The blue-glowing numbers read "10:31 p.m." A few hours earlier, she remembered, her apartment had been a violent storm. Her ex-husband had suddenly touched down there from out of nowhere — like some terrible tornado, twisting and turning and wreaking havoc in his path.

Then she remembered Rodney opening the back door, standing face to face with his father. At first, her son had been confused. But when he saw what this bad man had done to her, he turned into a miniature image of his menacing progenitor. Lashing out at his father with everything he had, Rodney tried to fight his way to his mother's side. But Sergeant Hudgins, laughing with that ugly guttural, animal sound that she had always hated, merely swatted him away like a fly, sending Rodney sprawling across the floor.

"Get up, boy, and try again. Let's see how much of yer daddy you got in ya!" Sergeant Hudgins had said, guffawing in near hysterics. He was enjoying the sport.

Rodney had tried again, and again he had gone down. His right temple scraped the corner of a bookshelf as he fell back. Forgetting her own beating moments earlier, Sally had scrambled across the floor toward her son. But her husband met her halfway, kicking the hard toe of his Dingo boot squarely into the side of her right cheek. The pain was so great that she had passed out.

She opened her eyes minutes later to see Rodney through the open door of a back bedroom, filling a brown-paper grocery sack with some of his clothes. Fearful for his mother's life, not to mention his own, her son was quietly obeying a string of orders from his father. Rodney's head hung low in defeat. The scrape on his temple still oozed dark blood.

"When you finish that, I want you to pack whatever road food y'all have got in the refrigerator. We're going on a little trip down below the gnat line."

"Don't take him, Jack! Don't take my boy!" she had cried out in vain.

"You forget, Sally, he's *our* boy, and I'm entitled to a little time with him."

Rodney continued his packing, listening but saying nothing. He was too scared.

"You had your chance. The judge gave you weekend visitation rights and you never came."

"And then you moved away so's I couldn't ever find you. So I reckon I've piled up a whole lot of weekend time with little Rodney since then. Besides, the boy's a whole lot better off with me. Look at this dump you're living in. You call this a home?"

"Why are you doing this, Jack?"

"'Cause I've decided that I need a son in my life. And 'cause Rodney's a whole lot better off with me. Look at the little bum. He's got hair down near his shoulders like some hippie trash. This boy needs discipline. He needs a father figure to get his butt in gear."

"Please don't hurt him, Jack."

"If he obeys his father, everything'll be all right. Ain't that right, boy?"

Rodney didn't answer.

"I said, ain't that right, boy! Did you hear me?"

"Yessir," Rodney finally answered, weakly.

Smiling, Sergeant Hudgins turned back toward his beaten wife and pointed a dirty-nailed finger at her. "And the same goes for you, Mrs. Hudgins. You keep to yourself and everything's all right. But so help me, if you try to follow me or call the police, I'll come back and kill you. I swear I will."

Still lying on the floor helplessly, she had watched her ex-husband send Rodney with his paper-sack suitcase out to the blue truck parked outside. For a moment, Rodney had thought about running into the night for help. But under the watchful eye of his captor, he had stopped short, fearing the consequences too much if he failed. Sitting defeated and alone on the passenger side of the musty-smelling truck, Rodney awaited his fate. He heard but did not see the rest of the destruction that unfolded back inside the apartment.

Sally Hudgins had made one last hopeless attempt to save her boy, lunging at her ex-husband with a dinner knife left on the living-room floor from the night before. She screamed in pain as he dodged her effort and grabbed a handful of hair from the back of her head. He twisted the mane in one fist and grabbed a single belt loop of her jeans with the other. Then he had thrown her like a sack of potatoes into the back bedroom. And now she remembered: Her head had slammed into a bedpost, apparently knocking her out.

Sitting now on the edge of her bed, she felt the crusty, sticky gash on the top of her head. Tears streamed down her cheeks in both sorrow and pain. What was she to do? Picking up the phone, she answered her own question. There was no other choice but to call the police. Her ex-husband had sworn he'd kill her, but she didn't care anymore. She only cared about her son.

✝ ✝ ✝

The U.S. Highway 27 road sign for Columbus, Georgia, read 31 miles when Sergeant Jack Hudgins spotted the first state trooper. He tensed at the thought that Sally might have contacted the authorities. His truck was traveling well below the speed limit, so there couldn't be any problem there. The trooper's car headlights drew closer in his rear-view mirror, and Hudgins studied the identifiable shadow of the siren bubble for any sign of life. After a few pregnant seconds, the trooper pulled into the passing lane, gunned the engine and sped down the road. Hudgins relaxed again.

Staring through the dark cabin of his truck, he looked at the sleeping figure of his young son on the seat beside him. With his stringy, long hair, the boy looked like some mangy dog. But I'll whip him into shape in no time, Hudgins thought to himself. Just like one of my recruits.

Several more minutes down the road, Hudgins' mind was still rambling aimlessly when he was jolted back to full attention at the sight of a blue flashing trooper light. A short distance ahead, two Georgia State Patrol cars were parked in a roadblock across the highway. He pressed his right foot down on the squeaky brake pedal, sending Rodney catapulting into the dashboard. Turning his head, Hudgins spotted another trooper car, lights flashing and closing in fast from behind.

"Get down, boy!" he ordered Rodney, who had pulled himself off the floorboard and onto his knees atop the seat. Rodney obeyed, crouching down while still wiping the sleep from his eyes.

The approaching trooper cruised slowly and carefully to a stop behind Hudgins' truck. The patrol car's lights still flashed wildly, coloring Hudgins' face in an eerie blue glow. The door of the car opened, and Hudgins saw a large figure step onto the pavement. The four vehicles — his truck and the three patrol cars ahead and behind him — sat in the middle of the lonely southbound lane of Highway 27 just outside the town of Hamilton. Hudgins squeezed his grip on the steering wheel and quickly ran through his options. The army had trained him to think fast in such a crisis.

As his decision clicked into place, he simultaneously released his left foot from the brake and stomped the right down hard on the truck's rubber-worn gas pedal. He pulled down hard on the left rung of the ribbed steering wheel, steering his vehicle into a skidding U-turn and nearly overturning in a ditch on the grassy shoulder of the road. The trooper cowered behind his own car for a few seconds to avoid being run over, then slid back inside the front seat, barking rapidly into his radio. Hudgins' truck raced back toward the tiny community of Pine Mountain.

Three miles later, Hudgins was alone again on the road. His eyes held their gaze on the highway as he reached down toward the dash. With one hand, he punched at a round knob, shutting off his headlights. Darkness fell around the truck. A moonlit stretch of straight highway lay before him, and he pushed down harder on the accelerator. The engine whined in protest, bucking and thumping like a wild horse; it paused for a few frozen seconds, then finally submitted to the driver's whip, slinging the truck faster into the night.

"What are you doing?" Rodney said, breaking his silence. He was shaking in terror.

"Shut up and go back to sleep!"

After gunning the truck flat out for another two miles and seventy seconds, Sergeant Hudgins gently eased back on the pedal, slowing the truck just enough to hang a perpendicular right onto an unmarked country road. The squealing tires threw loose rock under the truck bed, rattling so loud that Rodney feared the floorboard was coming apart.

"Ha, ha, ha-a-a-a! Try and catch me now, blue boys!"

Holding himself with both arms wrapped around his chest, Rodney squeezed harder into a tight ball as he cowered in fear on the dirty floorboard. Overhead in the dark sky, a small cloud dissipated, unleashing the full strength of the moon's reflected light. It briefly shone into the truck's dark cabin just bright enough to outline a profile of the driver's face.

It was at that moment that Rodney suddenly remembered the man beside him. Somewhere in the dark recesses of his subconscious, a fleeting wisp of memory flashed vividly in his mind's eye. The brutal laugh. The roughly carved face. Somewhere long ago, Rodney had heard and seen this ugly combination before. His mother had never said much about his father, and Rodney had never thought much about why he didn't have one. Now this crazy man beside him had suddenly broken into Rodney's home, beaten his mother, and said things like, "Ain't ya glad to see yer daddy?" Rodney still couldn't place the man's face, but now he remembered the badness. The meanness. The evil.

All at once, Rodney's panic swelled up in his chest and puddled his eyes with tears. He screamed in fright, grabbing for the passenger door handle without realizing it. The door cracked open an inch, then slammed back shut as the truck swerved in the road. A hairy hand clamped down on the back of Rodney's neck. Twisting, Rodney desperately tried to pull loose. He fought back like a crazed animal, eventually breaking free of the grasp and sliding his back against the passenger door. Immediately, he began kicking wildly at his father. The sole of his left tennis shoe missed once. The other foot jammed into the truck's A.M. radio, somehow turning on a country music station. For a split second, Sergeant Hudgins lost his concentration on both the road and his son as the loud rhythms of a slide guitar filled the cabin. The distraction was just enough to allow Rodney's third kick, unleashed from the muscles of his left thigh and shin, to connect squarely with the bottom of his father's jaw. The sergeant's face slapped hard against the glass of the closed window beside him. Pain shot across the bridge of his nose, squinting his eyes involuntarily.

"Idiot! What are ya doing!"

Rodney continued his furious attack, his feet now finding an unprotected target with each kick. Three more times Sergeant Hudgins felt his head bumped by the hard rubber edges of Rodney's shoes. Ignited by the stinging kicks, he released his right fist from the steering wheel and shoved it down hard into the side of Rodney's rib cage, knocking the boy violently into the floorboard.

The truck swerved wildly to the right. The sergeant instantly backed off the gas pedal but not in time to stop the vehicle from leaving the narrow road. A tall, skinny pine tree jumped out of the darkness and in front of his truck, but Hudgins never saw it. He only felt the impact, which slung him against the steering wheel and then rocketed him into and out the windshield. Tiny pieces of glass shattered behind him like a comet's tail as he hurtled through the night air.

Joint by joint, the truck's body crunched into accordion folds of metal, wrapping around and encasing Rodney in its rusty tomb. Still lying down in the passenger floorboard, Rodney was aware of nothing in the split second of the collision. The blackness around him only seemed to get darker, and then there was peace.

✛ ✛ ✛

Sally Hudgins learned the news about the crash from her hospital bed at Grady Memorial in downtown Atlanta. The painkillers had dulled her senses, but she immediately sat up straight when the Georgia State Patrol officer walked into her room.

"Mrs. Hudgins?"

"Yeah, that's me. Did you find my boy?" she asked groggily.

"Yes ma'am, we have."

"Oh, you have? You have? Is he all right?"

The officer looked down, searching for the right words. This job of mine, he thought, never gets easier.

"Ma'am, I'm sorry. But I'm afraid your husband ..."

"My ex-husband," she interrupted.

"Yes ma'am, your ex-husband. I'm sorry. I'm afraid that he and your son were involved in an accident off Highway 27 down near Callaway Gardens. Your ... ex-husband, Mr. Hudgins, didn't make it. I'm afraid he died. But it happened instantly."

"What about Rodney? What about my boy?" she said. Her eyes searched desperately for the answer in the patrolman's face.

"Yes, ma'am. They transported your son to a hospital in LaGrange. At the moment, I understand he's in some sort of a coma, but he's still alive."

"Rod ... ney! Rod ... ney!" she screamed loudly, sobbing at the same time in big gulps. "Rodney! No, no, no-o-o-o-o! My Rod ... ney-y-y-y-y-y!"

Two nurses rushed into the room at the sound of Sally's hysterics and attempted to calm her. The patrolman stepped back from the bed and closed the door, blocking the view from a few curious gawkers in the hallway.

"Mrs. Hudgins, please," one of the nurses said smoothly. "You're in no condition to be acting this way. Please try to calm yourself."

"Rod ... ney! Rod ... ney!" she continued to scream.

The door opened again and a white-jacketed doctor slipped inside with a hypodermic. Sally had to be held down physically by both nurses as the man administered the tranquilizer with a quick jab to her shoulder. Several minutes later, Rodney's name was still on her lips when the medication kicked in, sending her off — un-willingly — into a deep and troubled sleep.

✝ ✝ ✝

Rodney lay motionless beneath the single-bed sheet. He was hooked by several tiny clear tubes to an assortment of bottles and machines. But in his mind, he was free. And he was happy.

He dreamed of a large amusement park with bright lights and rides and games. A group of kids — he didn't recognize their faces but somehow knew them — stood beside him chattering in excite-ment.

"Which ride next, Rodney? What ya wanna ride next?"

Rodney smiled and looked around him. There was so much to choose from, but the giant Ferris wheel looked like the most fun.

"I think … I think that we'll do the Ferris wheel now," he said, beaming with delight.

"Yea-a-a-a-a-a-a!" the kids answered in choppy chorus as they turned in unison and ran. Rodney laughed and started to follow, but then he heard something faintly familiar in the night. He stopped, straining to hear over the loud din of a nearby shooting gallery.

"Rod … ney! Rod … ney!"

Somewhere far away, his mother was calling.

One of his friends turned around from a few yards away and cried out, "C'mon Rodney! Let's go!"

Rodney smiled, walking forward. Then he heard the voice again.

"Rod … ney! Rod … ney!" The voice was growing fainter, but its desperation could still be heard.

Rodney stopped again. He looked at his friends, then back over his shoulder at the darkness.

"Let's go, Rodney! The Ferris wheel, c'mon!"

Rodney looked back at his friends again and waved. He turned away, walking fast at first and then breaking into a run. His young arms chugging back and forth as fast as he could move them, he sprinted away from the lights and into the dark. And back to his mama.

Chapter Twenty-One

Never before had Eddie experienced so many ups and downs in such a brief span. It was as if his emotions were strung to a giant yo-yo. Since departing Big Oak Ranch, there had been the incredible high of the Vince Dooley meeting. Then loneliness and rejection had crept in as his time ran out at Ignatius House. From out of nowhere, divine intervention brought David Salyers and a new place to live. A succession of other small victories had followed with his talk before the large crowd at Metro Bible Study and the offering of wise guidance from a kingpin in Georgia banking. But now, as the Christmas season of 1982 drew nearer, he was spinning back down again.

Eddie still clung to a thread of hope, but it was difficult with a weakening physical condition that did little to sustain his enthusiasm. He was tired — a state of body and mind that was exacerbated because of so little to show for all his hard work. He was a little hungry, too. Eddie's weight had dropped from 210 down to less than 180 pounds — not much meat on a six-foot five-inch frame. The belt-looped waistband of one pair of jeans had been taken up so many times that his two back pockets nearly touched when he wore them.

Eddie was not exactly homeless, but he was close to facing the possibility. Down to just fifty dollars in his checking account, he was rationing meals with a diet of cheese, crackers and milk. He had long ago decided not to ask his mother or his grandfather for any more money. This was his and God's battle, not theirs. Lately, however, he was beginning to suspect that it wasn't really God's battle either. Indeed, he was becoming increasingly skeptical.

One evening, after an especially discouraging day of no tangible progress, Eddie returned exhausted to the house in Powder Springs, collapsing onto a couch. His stomach growled with hunger but there was nothing there to eat. Sighing, he tried not to think about eating. He could make it till morning, then splurge on a two-dollar McDonald's breakfast.

"God, you've made a fool out of me!" Eddie said out loud with anger. Lying on his back, he stared at the ceiling, almost as if in a daze. Glistening traces of tears rimmed the lids of his eyes. "What am I going to do?" he asked — half-talking to God, half-talking to himself. "I left everything for You and here I am with one week's worth of money. So now, it looks like I'm heading back to Alabama a failure. Is that how you want it?"

He swung his legs off the couch and moved into a sitting position, his hands clasped between his knees. In a much calmer voice, he whispered hoarsely, "I've done all that I know that I can do. I've been here almost six months, and I'm no further along than when I left Big Oak. This is going to be humiliating. I've talked to too many people about Eagle Ranch … What are they going to think now?"

Eddie shook his head back and forth. He closed his eyes and shut his mouth. Darkness settled into the room as the frail light of an impending winter diminished outside. The living room went silent as he began to pray inside his head.

"Lord, I don't want to quit. But I'm not sure that you're in this anymore. If you are, I need to see something … some sort of sign, or else I'm heading back home."

He sighed, finished a few more prayer requests, then rose to head for the bathroom to brush his teeth. It was only 8 p.m., but he was ready to hit the sack. A few minutes later, he was in his bedroom and under the covers. "One more week," he said to himself before dozing off. "I'll give it one more week." Already, he was beginning to consider his options. He could follow back up on an earlier job opportunity as a sports physiologist with the respected Cooper's Clinic in Dallas, Texas. Or, there was always teaching and coaching again. ... Sleep overtook him before he could ponder anything more.

✢ ✢ ✢

Eddie rose early the next morning, a Wednesday, after a surprisingly restful night. He felt a little guilt left over from his frustration the night before, but he wasn't second-guessing his self-imposed deadline as he settled down on his knees to pray beside his bed. His first appointment that day wasn't until 10 a.m. He could take his time.

His morning prayer had hardly begun when the telephone interrupted. He let it ring several times before reaching up to the table beside his bed to unsaddle the receiver.

"Hello?"

The voice on the other end of the line paused before answering. "Is this Eddie Staub?"

"Yes it is." The man sounded familiar, but Eddie couldn't quite place him.

"Eddie, this is Loyd Strickland."

Loyd Strickland, Loyd Strickland ... Eddie's mind raced; then he remembered — the man with Crystal Farms up in Gainesville. I wonder how he got my phone number, Eddie thought to himself before answering.

"Yes sir, Mr. Strickland. How are you?"

"Fine, fine," he replied cordially. "Eddie, what are you doing right now?"

"To tell you the truth, I've been praying."

"Well, listen here, you get off those knees of yours right now."

"What?"

"I said get off of your knees. I've decided to give you $10,000 through my foundation, and there's another fella up here who'll probably give you $5,000 more — that is, if you can find the time in your busy schedule to make it up here to talk to him. So get up and start moving, son. I believe you've got some work to do."

Chapter Twenty-Two

On December 22, 1982, Eddie Staub moved on an act of faith to the Poultry Capital of the World. He was convinced now that somewhere in Hall County, Georgia, lay the future of Eagle Ranch. No fewer than a half-dozen local Realtors were now enlisted under Eddie's direction to zero in on a suitable 100- to 200-acre tract somewhere within Hall County's borders.

Through the help of a local philanthropist, Rosemary Dodd — she was married to Ed Dodd, a nationally syndicated cartoonist and creator of the Mark Trail comic strip — Eddie had found free living quarters at a home for cancer victims and other patients receiving treatment at the nearby Northeast Georgia Medical Center. Rarely were there any vacancies at the House of Grace, but Eddie had been fortunate again — at least for the time being. He was getting accustomed to living life one day at a time.

Prior to finding his new base, Eddie had asked one of his Realtor contacts, Verla Smith of Gainesville, to be on the lookout for a cheap place to stay. Within a week, Verla came back to him with a steal: a tiny downtown Gainesville apartment for seventy-five dollars a month.

"I'm afraid that's a little out of my price range," Eddie had confessed. "I hope you didn't go to too much trouble."

"Excuse me for asking this," the Realtor had responded politely, "but how do you plan to buy the land that we're looking for?"

His hands stuffed inside the two pockets of his jeans, Eddie had merely shrugged his shoulders, smiled, and answered, "I haven't quite figured that one out yet."

It had been more than six months since Eddie had met with Vince Dooley. Since then, the University of Georgia coach had come through on one of two promises. He had opened the door to Rankin Smith, one of the state's most prominent and generous sports figures. Eddie's meeting with Smith, owner of the Atlanta Falcons, had been cordial enough. However, Smith had openly expressed doubts as to whether Eddie could ever make Eagle Ranch happen.

With the end of the University of Georgia football season, Dooley now worked on his other promise: Fran Tarkenton. A legendary quarterback for Georgia in the late 1950s and a professional Hall of Fame star with the Minnesota Vikings, Tarkenton had been equally adept in his transition to the business world. He currently operated a profitable computer-software firm based in Atlanta in addition to overseeing and directing numerous other successful investments.

Dooley paved the way for an initial contact with Tarkenton by phone. Eddie had grown up watching Tarkenton scramble out of the pocket and pull out numerous come-from-behind wins for the Vikings on television. Now here Eddie was in the humble surroundings of the House of Grace listening to this superstar actually talking to him from the other end of a telephone line. Eddie was more than a little excited. His heart pumped fast and the hairs on the back of his neck seemed to stand up on their ends. He was in awe.

"Eddie, I've heard about your project from Coach Dooley, and it sounds exciting," Tarkenton said. His voice was instantly recognizable.

"Thank you. I'd like to …"

Tarkenton interrupted. "Eddie, tell you what I want you to do. I want you to get in touch with my business associate Marvin

Bluestein. I'll give you his phone number in a minute. You call him, go over all the details with Marvin, and he'll fill me in. Then, we'll see whether we need to get together."

"Okay, that sounds great to me. I appreciate your time and anything that you can do to help out," Eddie said.

"You bet. Now I'm going to put my secretary on the line, and she'll get you a phone number for Marvin."

"Yes sir. Thank you."

A week later, Eddie went through the first of what would become a succession of hurdles on the way toward a face-to-face meeting with Tarkenton. He met with Tarkenton's adviser, Marvin Bluestein, in a sixteenth-floor office of the dominant Tower Place skyscraper in the Lenox Square area of north Atlanta. It was headquarters for the Tarkenton Group, the holding company for the celebrity's various companies and investments.

Although he stood only four inches over five feet tall, Bluestein was an intimidating-looking man who wore dark suits and a stern, all-business manner. Despite first impressions, Eddie found him to be immediately affable and even more than a little interested in Eagle Ranch. Bluestein also was very detailed, asking a series of pointed questions about the proposed boys' ranch, including funding sources, operational philosophy, various needs, and Eddie's qualifications to run the ranch. Eddie answered the questions as best he could, searching his inquisitor's eyes after each answer for some clue to his reaction. Bluestein was impenetrable, wearing a firm countenance throughout their meeting.

After an hour, Bluestein seemed satisfied. Rising from his leather office chair, he extended a hand, signaling a close to their session. He asked Eddie to call back in three weeks to report his progress. It seemed a long time to wait, but Eddie didn't press. Tarkenton's involvement in the ranch might be the answer to his prayers, and he didn't want to mess it up.

In the days that followed, Eddie toured every nook and cranny of Hall County in search of the perfect spot. Rejuvenated with a real sense of God's involvement, he spent the time looking ahead to such details as how the first boys' home and an administration building should look. The generous donation of time from a few local architects allowed him to begin putting his vision to paper. Operational details, which up to that point had been stored in his head, were being written down as well. Now that he had identified the general location of Eagle Ranch, he needed to paint a more definitive picture for potential donors.

He proudly presented the preliminary drawings of the first boys' home along with several pages documenting his progress to Bluestein during their second meeting in late January of 1983. Scanning through the documents while Eddie watched from across his desk, Bluestein still gave no hint of what he was thinking. Their meeting was much shorter than the first, and Eddie was asked to report back in another two weeks.

The routine repeated itself with a third meeting, a fourth, and so on throughout the winter. Privately, Bluestein was impressed with Eddie's perseverance. And despite his busy schedule with numerous other Tarkenton Group projects, he actually began to look forward to seeing Eddie at each opportunity. He had to admit that he liked the guy and even felt his motives were pure. Still, he had to approach the Eagle Ranch proposal like any other business deal. Bluestein had been involved with another children's home several years earlier in Brunswick, Georgia, that initially looked promising but later encountered innumerable problems. To Bluestein's way of thinking, there was no doubt that Eddie had the desire. But did he have the stamina to keep the donor money rolling in for the ranch several years down the road?

Five meetings later, Eddie was still hanging on — never protesting and always demonstrating a little more progress. Bluestein had a hunch that Eddie wasn't going away. It was time to meet with Fran.

Eddie returned to the high-rise Atlanta offices of the Tarkenton Group on the following Friday. This time, he was led into a nicely furnished conference room and seated across from Bluestein at one corner of a long glass-top table. A female secretary offered refreshments but Eddie politely declined. He was too nervous.

For the first few minutes, it was the two of them, just like the last several sessions that had led to this one. Eddie engaged in small talk with Bluestein, all the while wondering whether Tarkenton would really show. A door clicked. Turning halfway in his seat, Eddie saw the familiar face of Fran Tarkenton enter the room. To have been such a giant in the world of sports, the man looked shorter than Eddie had imagined. Still, his presence filled the room. Though unnecessary, Bluestein introduced his boss, and from that point on, he let Tarkenton take command.

"Okay, Eddie. It's good to finally meet you in person. Let's get straight to the point — I understand you're making some headway on your boys' ranch project," Tarkenton said. He was all business.

"Yes sir," Eddie answered, hoping the quiver in his voice couldn't be detected.

"Well, why don't you run through it for me to get us started?"

Eddie became calmer as he ran through his spiel. So many times had he pitched the ranch that he could have done it in his sleep — and probably had. First, he laid out the strong need for a boys' home in Northeast Georgia, supporting it with copies of letters from juvenile court judges and other related state authorities. Victor Gregory's continued counsel had helped him improve his homework, and the resulting documentation was impressive. He then discussed his background at Big Oak, his master's degree, and teaching experience. Finally, he painted a picture of the ranch operations, both in philosophy and physical appearance. Trying so hard to impress his audience, however, Eddie didn't realize he was taking way too much time. Tarkenton was beginning to steal glances at his watch. A busy man, he was not interested in details. He wanted the big picture.

"Hold on, Eddie," he said, stopping the monologue. "Marvin's gone over all of this with me. What do you see as my role?"

Eddie responded without hesitation. "I want you to help me raise $250,000 and be on my board of advisers."

"All right, well here's what I think. I'd like to be totally involved. I want to be on your executive committee, not just your advisory board. And the money is no problem. I can sell this thing in one day. We'll set up a meeting at the Capital City Club, and you'll get your $250,000. Don't worry about that."

Eddie suppressed the makings of a wide grin, not wanting to give himself away. He hadn't expected such a positive response. In fact, he had never been so well received by any potential donor — particularly in terms of discussing actual dollars for the ranch. "That's great, Fran. Just great."

"Well, don't get your hopes up quite yet. There are still some details to work out, but this looks good," said Tarkenton. He glanced momentarily at his associate as if to say, "Did I promise too much?"

Still a little unsure as to what had transpired, Eddie pressed gently for a more definitive answer. "Fran, if you don't mind, where do you think we go from here?"

"Like I said, I've got a few things to talk over with Marvin, and then we'll get in touch with you soon."

"Great! Thanks, Fran. I'm really excited about this."

"Sure thing, Eddie."

Walking through the Tower Place parking garage to his car, Eddie was tempted to let out a big whoop. But he stopped short, reminding himself not to get his hopes up. "Let's make sure he calls me back first," he said to himself as he scooted behind the driver's wheel of his Toyota. After leaving the garage, he traveled the three-mile jaunt along Lenox Road to Interstate 85 North and then floated the rest of the way back to Gainesville.

✛ ✛ ✛

Less than a week after the Tarkenton meeting, Eddie received a call from Bluestein on the communal phone in the main downstairs hallway of the House of Grace. They exchanged the usual pleasantries, which stretched for only a few seconds, before a brief pause fell between them. Eddie held his breath in anticipation. Was the deal with Tarkenton off?

"Eddie, I have some great news for you," Bluestein said. "We've found the perfect spot for Eagle Ranch."

The words hit Eddie like a thunderbolt. Without realizing it, he stood up from the old wooden chair in which he was seated. "Where is it, Marvin?"

"It's on Carter's Lake — a beautiful piece of property. You're going to love it."

"Where is Carter's Lake? Is it in Northeast Georgia?"

"No, Eddie, it's not. It's more to the west, near Ellijay, which is still in north Georgia — just not exactly where you were looking."

Eddie sat back down again, rubbing his forehead. The need for a boys' home in that part of the state was nowhere as critical as it was in Northeast Georgia. The pronouncement hadn't quite burst his bubble, but it had deflated it a little. He had been so sure of his present course.

"Eddie, let's not make any decisions on the phone. I want you to see this property first. I'm pretty confident you'll be pleased."

The land covered eighty acres of woods in the mountains north of the Georgia town of Ellijay, well-known for its apple orchards. Carter's Lake, which sat in the middle of the tract, was the deepest man-made lake in the United States. Officials with the Tarkenton Group had come up with a plan to let the boys at Eagle Ranch run a marina to assist with operational money. They also intended to purchase the property — allowing the ranch to spend its dollars on kids instead of interest payments. Tom Joiner, a Tarkenton Group attorney, put Eddie in touch with an Ellijay land broker — who happened to be Joiner's brother — and a tour of the property was scheduled for the following Saturday morning.

As promised, it was spectacular. The lake, the mountains, even the nearby streets of small-town Ellijay — the combination was as pretty as any mountain resort. Had it all been located in Hall County, it would have been perfect, Eddie thought. But unfortunately, it wasn't.

Driving back to Gainesville that Saturday afternoon, Eddie dreaded his next conversation with Bluestein. He could tell that Bluestein was truly excited over finding the property. And after months of having doors closed in his face, here was somebody no less than Fran Tarkenton offering to join his mission. He had even gone so far as to pick out a land site and offer to pay for it. How could he possibly turn that down?

Eddie still hadn't made up his mind what to say later that evening when the main-hallway phone rang at the House of Grace. Someone downstairs called Eddie's name. Slowly emerging from his room, where he was starting to prepare for bed, Eddie took his time walking down the stairs to answer the call. Picking up the receiver, he said hello and immediately recognized the voice that answered on the other end. It was Bluestein.

"Eddie, looks like you guys had a beautiful day. What did you think?"

"Marvin, you were right. It is some of the prettiest land that I have ever seen," Eddie answered, attempting to soften his next words. "But ... uh ..."

"Wait a minute, Eddie. I'm guessing that you still might have some reservations because of the location and this deal about being in an 'area of need.' But before you make up your mind, let me tell you something that you need to weigh into that equation. Build Eagle Ranch at Carter's Lake, and I promise you: You'll never have to worry about where the operational money is going to come from. We'll help you take care of that."

"That's very generous, Marvin."

"Now, wait, hear me out some more. ... I know that your biggest concern is the location, but why not look at it from another perspective, Eddie. It's so isolated — what a perfect sheltering place for kids to escape to, and for you and your staff to concentrate on helping them through their pain. The location really is an advantage."

"Marvin, I just don't see it that way. I'm sorry," said Eddie, butting into the one-way conversation before the avalanche went too far. "Eagle Ranch has got to be in an area of need or there's no real purpose. You know there already are things in place over in northwest Georgia. There's nothing up here in the Gainesville area."

"Okay, Eddie." Bluestein's voice did not mask his feelings. He was disappointed. He had just offered the opportunity of a lifetime

— a chance for Eddie to declare an end to his trials and a victory for his Lord. But Eddie wasn't budging.

"I'm sorry, Marvin. But look, we're real close to finding something up here, so please don't give up on me."

"Eddie, I'll tell you the way I feel. If you think you can come up with something better, then you should move on it quickly. We can't sit on a deal like this, because it won't be around forever, okay?"

"I understand, Marvin."

"Keep in touch."

Eddie slowly placed the phone back in its cradle on a folding card table and leaned back in the table's cheap accessory, a hard wooden chair. He began to ponder what he had just said and done. Marvin was right about one thing. Eddie could put an end to all his worries about letting down God in front of so many witnesses. The Carter's Lake property and Fran Tarkenton's involvement would be viewed as a tremendous accomplishment for Eddie to have pulled off. Still, Eddie knew deep in his heart that God had led him to Northeast Georgia, where kids who needed help had no place nearby to go. He appreciated Tarkenton's offer, but he couldn't let the man's generosity steer him away from his original direction and gut feeling about the future of the ranch.

On Fran's behalf, Eddie vowed to step up his search for a suitable land site in Hall County. He still saw Fran's influence and support as vital for the ranch's future, and he would work hard to keep him in his corner. That night, Eddie prayed for guidance. And as he rolled over to sleep in his bed, oddly, he felt at peace.

Chapter Twenty-Three

Eddie found what he was looking for in early March of 1983 — just a few weeks after his last conversation with Marvin Bluestein of the Tarkenton Group. The land was in south Hall County in the rural community of Chestnut Mountain. The path to the site followed a winding stretch of asphalt called Union Church Road that was bordered by several country homes, beautiful white-picket fences, mobile-home trailers, and numerous cattle and horse farms.

The Mulberry River cut through the middle of a 900-acre tract of land that once was the beating heart of the south Hall community. It now looked abandoned with an old rusty barn and a crumbling former homestead that still contained old kitchen utensils and other signs of a life that once was. The property was being held as part of the estate of the late J. Alton Hosch, a former dean of the Lumpkin School of Law at the University of Georgia. His widow, Nina Rusk Hosch, was co-executrix of the estate along with Bank South in Atlanta.

It was as if the land had been sitting there waiting for Eddie to bump into it. Everything that he had envisioned about Eagle Ranch was there: a river and a perfect site for a lake where boys could fish, swim and simply be boys; a ranch setting where horses could be raised and fed by the kids; and a bucolic serenity buffered by a thick forest of pines and oaks. Despite the property's seclusion, it was only a few minutes from a major interstate highway that provided easy access from Northeast Georgia to metro Atlanta. About the only negative was a tall radio tower under construction at the south-western edge of the property. Eddie could only rationalize that it must be God's way of marking the site. Later, he would learn that the tower was the only thing that even kept the price of the land within reach.

As Eddie had woven his way through the small-town connections that criss-cross a community like Gainesville, he had befriended a respected local attorney, Frank Armstrong, who possessed a weakness for noble causes. A teddy-bearish man with a gruff voice, Armstrong early on had offered to help Eddie in any way that he could. Eddie now decided to put him to the test. He needed someone with credibility to represent his interest in buying a 180-acre slice of the Hosch property.

Armstrong gladly accepted Eddie's request and promptly contacted a Decatur attorney, James Mackay, who represented the family heir to the estate. A former U.S. congressman and the son of a Methodist minister, Mackay politely told Armstrong that though the project sounded admirable he could not commit to anything until first talking to the heir and the bank. Privately, Mackay was doubtful the deal would ever happen. The real-estate market was slow, interest rates were sky-high, and the bank was listening to any and all of the few inquiries about the property. But in order to settle the Hosch estate, the bank would want cash up front. Mackay also knew the project had scarce funding, and no financial institution — no matter how great the cause — was about to lend a large sum of money to an altruistic project with the likelihood of foreclosure down the road.

Mackay's intuition proved to be on the mark. Bob Russell, the bank's trust executive in charge of the estate, was far from interested when contacted by the Hosch family attorney. "Jim," Russell had told him by phone, "you know I've got better things to do than talk to young dreamers. I admire what the guy is trying to do, but my client has to come first. Furthermore, the prime market period is due to return in a few months, and I don't want to risk having the property tied up in negotiations that take us nowhere."

Considering the case closed, Mackay had followed up the next day with Armstrong. The bank, as Mackay expected, simply was not interested.

Armstrong well understood the circumstances — Eddie Staub was probably the poorest business risk in north Georgia — but the Gainesville lawyer wasn't willing to give up so easily. Knowing Eddie's personable nature and strong gift for persuasion, Armstrong felt there still might be a chance if Eddie were to meet directly with the family heir. Perhaps, Armstrong speculated, emotion could win over reason. Eddie harbored the same hope.

"God, you can change the minds of kings," Eddie prayed, "and I know you can change the minds of these people who hold the land."

It was a prayer that Eddie prayed every night for several weeks after finding the land along the Mulberry River. Despite the bank's cold shoulder, Eddie's heart told him that he had found a home for Eagle Ranch. Taking Frank Armstrong's advice, he attempted to reach the land's heir by phone and through the mail. His initial efforts failed to prompt a response, but Eddie vowed to keep on trying. In the meantime, he went about his business as if the land were already his, walking and studying the property from every angle imaginable. With the help of a local soil conservation specialist, Johnny Mattox, he pored over a topographical map and pinpointed a spot to dam the river for a small lake. Then, he enlisted the help of a local surveyor, Don Canupp, to produce a site plan from the topo. Eddie hoped that doing his homework in such a professional manner would impress the bank and the Hosch family heir, and demonstrate his resolve.

After several more persistent phone calls and letters, he finally received a break. Nina Hosch and her bank representative agreed to meet with him at the office of her attorney, James Mackay, in downtown Decatur to discuss drawing property lines for the section of land that Eddie was after. "But don't get your hopes up, Mr. Staub," she had said by phone. "This will be merely a fact-finding mission for the record, and I must tell you that my attorney is very skeptical at this point."

Even if it wasn't a "yes," Eddie was elated nonetheless. He was still in the running — for now. And for now, he would keep praying and hoping that God would spawn a miracle in the woods of Chestnut Mountain.

✝ ✝ ✝

Nina Rusk Hosch was the first cousin of former U.S. Secretary of State Dean Rusk, but she was better known for her own list of remarkable accomplishments. A prominent educator, she was the first dean of women at Emory University near Decatur, her hometown. Her life had been spent throughout the world as a member of the Army Nurse Corps during World War II and later as a Peace Corps foreign service officer. Mrs. Hosch was sixty-nine years old. Her face was lined and her hair was gray, but she had the vitality of a much younger woman. She remained very active in community affairs, particularly in those dealing with Emory University and its nursing school.

When Eddie finally met face to face with the woman at her attorney's office, he immediately felt at ease in her presence. Despite her great community stature, there was not a trace of arrogance or elitism in her down-home manner. Eddie thought about how much he would have preferred to have met with her all alone; it was going to be difficult dividing his energy and focus between her and her two advisers, James Mackay and Bob Russell of Bank South. To shore up his own side, Eddie had asked Frank Armstrong to join him at the afternoon meeting.

Mackay, wearing a pair of bifocals pushed up atop his balding head, gestured to a round table surrounded by several wooden chairs, and one by one the small group found their seats. A glass wall on one side of the room revealed the picturesque and historic DeKalb County Courthouse and its well-manicured green lawns outside.

"Okay, folks, is everyone comfortable?" asked Mackay, ever the Southern gentleman. "Then let's get started. Mr. Staub, why don't you start us off by telling a little bit about yourself. And then I think it would be helpful if you go over what you have in mind with the J. Alton Hosch property and exactly how you propose to finance the purchase."

Eddie paused before answering. He cleared his throat, stalling briefly to mentally organize his thoughts. Then he began by describing his experience at Big Oak Ranch and his subsequent heart's desire to start his own children's home. As he spoke, he involuntarily pressed the ends of his fingers together, conveying a cogent spirit of faith and determination to his audience. Russell, who had been told of Eddie's college baseball career, couldn't help but wonder why the guy wasn't instead pursuing a professional sports contract of some kind. It still might be a long shot, Russell thought, but it sure would be a whole heck of a lot easier than this boys' home project.

"This is what I want to do," Staub said, concluding his remarks as if to answer Russell's thoughts. "And we feel sure of the need and that we can succeed."

Mrs. Hosch was the first to respond. Displaying a warm smile and twinkling eyes — Eddie thought she looked like the perfect Mrs. Santa Claus — she reeled off a series of pointed questions in regard to Eagle Ranch and its goals. She seemed genuinely interested, and despite their differences in age, an easy rapport seemed to have settled in between her and Eddie. She spoke to him like she would her own grandson but with an underlying tone of strictly business. The balance was a message to Eddie that she might be sympathetic to his mission but she wasn't going to literally "sell the farm" on emotion alone.

Russell and Mackay conducted their own inquiries, then ended the meeting with a round of handshakes and a poker-face promise to give full consideration to Eddie's proposal. Mackay escorted Eddie and Frank Armstrong to a main elevator, while Russell and his client hung back in Mackay's office. A few minutes later, Mackay returned, closing the door behind him. The three returned to their seats around the conference table.

"Okay, Nina, Bob ... What do you think?"

"Jim, you know on paper that this is crazy. That boy has nothing to show us but a dream," Russell answered, rocking back in his chair.

"I know that. But you've got to admit that the kid is sincere, and he seems to have picked up quite a bit of community support up there in Gainesville," Mackay answered.

"Gentlemen," Mrs. Hosch said, commanding their attention. "I don't know whether he can succeed or not, but something moves me not to stand in the way. There's something different about this project, almost like a spiritual force is behind Mr. Staub."

The two men nodded out of respect, then deftly shifted the conversation back to an analysis of the facts.

"Bob, let me ask you this," Mackay said. "Are there any other parties at all interested in the property?"

"Just one. And they're bottom fishing for sure. The real estate market is just dead in the water right now. I wouldn't have even given this Staub guy the slightest look if we had a few more prospects — but there's really nobody."

"Your main concern is tying up the land?"

"Sure. They're offering to buy it for $144,000, which is reasonable, but Mr. Staub says he's raised only $15,000. I'm not about to jeopardize the settling of this estate while we wait around for him to come up with the rest of the money. The prime real-estate season is just two months away. Besides, this is not the time to be raising money for a project of this magnitude. The economy is too slow. Mr. Staub is going duck hunting when the ducks aren't flying, and I have serious concerns as to whether he can ever pull it off."

"I don't agree," Nina interjected. "Listen, I fully realize that this is a long shot, but I'd still like to give the boy a chance."

The room fell silent for several minutes as the two men privately pondered their predicament. Usually a no-nonsense person, Mrs. Hosch was clearly moved, and her eyes told them to find a way.

Russell sighed, then smiled at his client. "Okay, okay. Here's what I think we should do," he said, sitting straight up with a sense of affirmation. "We know this guy has good intentions, right? Well, let's test him."

Mackay removed his bifocals and leaned across the table closer to listen more intently. He was curious.

"I wonder if the boy's willing to put up all the money that he's raised so far, his entire $15,000, as earnest money. In return, we'll give him an option to buy the property over a period of no more than four months. If that scares him off, then we'll know. We'll know he would never have had the gumption to pull off a children's home in the first place."

✢ ✢ ✢

Eddie learned of the bank's decision a few days later in a phone call from Russell. He felt himself holding his breath as he awaited the verdict.

"Mr. Staub, the bank and Mrs. Hosch have agreed to grant you an option to buy the 180 acres that you have requested," the banker said, matter of factly. "But due to our strong concerns over whether you can come up with the necessary funding, we have set down the following conditions: First, you mentioned that you had raised approximately $15,000 on behalf of Eagle Ranch. We would expect that you put up this entire sum as nonrefundable earnest money. And second, our conditions are that you raise the remainder of our asking price of $144,000 in a 120-day time frame. If you do not come up with this sum by closing, then you would forfeit the $15,000 earnest money to the bank. And I trust that you understand that this would be only fair since we would be taking the property off the market for the four months prior to closing."

One hundred and twenty days! How in the world am I going to come up with that kind of money in such a short time, Eddie thought as the words sank in.

"Mr. Staub? Are you still there?"

"Yeah. Uh, I'm sorry. Yes sir. Uh, does that figure match the $800 an acre price that we offered?" Eddie was floored. He couldn't think of anything else to say.

"Yes, it does, and let me tell you that despite our restrictive terms, the bank is still very reluctant to even go this far. It is only the generosity of Mrs. Hosch and her strong feelings about your project that even brought us to this compromise."

"Yes sir. Oh, thank you, and I'll be sure to thank Mrs. Hosch. But let me be sure that I understand you correctly. You're wanting me to come up with $144,000 in cash?"

"That's right. And in 120 days — or no deal."

Chapter Twenty-Four

Rodney Hudgins was more than halfway through seventh grade — for the second time. He had been held back once before in DeKalb County. Now he was trying again at Buford Middle School, a small public school in a tiny town that straddled a county line and possessed a split personality wavering between rural backwoods and an emerging city. Buford, Georgia, lay forty minutes to the north of Atlanta, off Interstate 985.

It had been more than five years since Rodney's abduction and near death at the hands of his late father. Both he and his mother had fully recovered from their separate but connected fates. And life was finally looking up — at least for Rodney's mother. Sally had found herself a man.

Meeting by chance one night after work at an Atlanta bar, the pair had instantly hit it off. A few weeks later, Sally moved — with Rodney in stubborn tow — into the mobile home of her boyfriend, a local plumber, in Buford. She had quickly been able to find a decent job waiting tables at a diner there. And in a good week of tips, her pay often exceeded what she had earned at the cannery back in

Decatur. The work was tiring and tough on her back, but she was content for now. More important, she was in love. The horror of her other life was finally beginning to fade. Now, she thought to herself, if I could just get Rodney straightened out.

But in the wake of the move, Rodney had been far from controllable. Already that spring of 1983, he had managed to jump into two different scrapes with some of the kids living around the trailer park.

His body had mended fairly well since the truck crash — at least on the outside — but the accident had left him with several scars, one particularly nasty one in the left corner of his mouth. It had taken several stitches to repair a deep cut, and the resulting scar had left his top lip curled down slightly in a half-frown. Plastic surgery might have corrected it, but Sally's lack of health-care insurance had allowed only the basic care afforded to indigents. Besides having that scar, Rodney limped slightly. His left leg had been broken in three places. Together, the scar and limp served his peers as excellent fodder for making fun of the new kid at school.

"Fight'n — that's the only thing Rodney's good at is fight'n," said Wayne, Sally's new companion. It hadn't taken him long to grow tired of having the boy around. He wished Sally hadn't come with strings attached.

"Please, Wayne," she said one evening after Rodney's return to the trailer with another bloody nose and ripped T-shirt. "He's been through so much."

"Don't give me that crap, Sally. You said he got in a lot of fights back in Atlanta before all that kidnapping mess happened. That boy just needs a little discipline, that's all."

"But Wayne, his daddy beat him when he was just a little baby. Just give him time. I think he'll settle down after a while, once he gets used to living here and makes some friends."

"All I'm saying is that you shouldn't be giving the boy too much slack. He's playing you like a darn fiddle."

Later that night, as Sally tucked her son into bed, Wayne sat back in his TV-watching recliner and thought about Rodney. He vowed to resort to his belt the next time Rodney crossed the line. That's the way Wayne's father had done it. "My old man used to wear me out with that thing," he said under his breath, rubbing his stubby beard while thinking back to a few painful memories of childhood. "Now I guess it's my turn — time for me to wear Sally's boy out."

It wasn't long before that time came. A few days later, the Buford Middle School principal sent him home after a big fight with two other boys. Sally was tied up with the diner's busy lunch crowd, so she had to call Wayne away from a customer's leaky faucet to drive Rodney home for the day.

"The kids, they was a making fun of me. Said I've got a peg leg," Rodney said, pleading his case to Wayne on the way home.

"Young man, I had to miss out on a plumbing job 'cause of your little troublemaking. And let me tell you something else. You sure have been getting off mighty light with your mother on account of your poor little accident. But hey, I don't believe that crap. And now, boy, I'm going to do what she should have done a long time ago. I'm going to get you back to the trailer and whip your butt good. How does that sound?"

Rodney fell silent in the car, smoldering. He hated Wayne. He thought about how hard he had begged and pleaded with his mother not to move in with him. But she hadn't listened. All she could talk about was making "a new life" for their new family.

For Rodney, though, there was nothing different about his life, except that it was worse than ever. Back in the trailer, as he pulled down his pants and braced for his beating, Rodney thought about something for the first time. Very calmly and deliberately, ... he thought about how he would go about killing himself.

A HUNDRED AND TWENTY DAYS

Chapter Twenty-Five

April 1983

Since his journey to Georgia nine months earlier, Eddie Staub had traveled down a road that had been crumbling apart and growing dangerously narrower with each day. Along the way, he had faced the prospect of living out of his car. He had been down to one week's worth of money. And he had come within only a few days of giving up and packing for home. Each time, he somehow had found a way to pull himself back, at the last possible moment, from the edge.

In April of 1983, though, Eddie now very clearly faced the end of his precarious journey. Exactly 120 days would now determine the fate of Eagle Ranch if he decided to accept the bank's challenge to raise the required $144,000 for the land on Chestnut Mountain. A loan was out of the question. Except for the money from an occasional substitute-teaching job, he was practically penniless. It was ironic that Eddie was attempting to provide shelter for forty needy boys when he hardly had a roof over his own head. Only

Gainesville's small-town generosity kept him properly fed and housed.

After the phone call from Bank South, Eddie struggled for days over his next move. Was he gambling with the future of forty boys who had no say in the matter? More and more, the Fran Tarkenton offer in northwest Georgia seemed to be the obvious and safest route. Still, that would be shutting the door in Northeast Georgia, where he was sure God had led him.

In the end, though, Eddie decided not to base the land decision on his own feelings, the Tarkenton Group, or anyone else. It would be God's decision. In his heart, he truly believed that God had inspired him to start Eagle Ranch and that it should be located where it was needed most. With that rationale settled in his mind, Eddie came to the final conclusion that he had no other choice. Somehow, he would find a way to raise more than $1,000 a day by August 18, 1983. Somehow, he would find one more miracle.

✛ ✛ ✛

The Eagle Ranch bank account fell to zero on April 18, the date that Eddie signed a contract outlining the terms for the sale of the Chestnut Mountain property. He was joined in Jim Mackay's office by three new Eagle Ranch board members from Gainesville: businessman Roger Brown, and attorneys John Cromartie Jr. and Frank Armstrong. Present on the seller's side were Bob Russell of Bank South, Nina Hosch, and her attorney, Mackay.

The mood within the room was stilted. A few feeble stabs at a joke and small talk attempted to lighten the tension, but the air retained a distinct feeling of morbid business. Privately, Russell was perplexed. He never thought in a million years that this meeting would take place — not with these terms. At the same time, he felt a strong empathy for Eddie. *The boy obviously has good intentions and a strong faith,* Russell thought. *But this deal's simply never going to fly.*

After the signing, Eddie took his copies of the legal documents and, driving alone, headed up I-85 and the I-985 connector to the Chestnut Mountain property forty-five minutes away. His mud-stained Toyota kicked up a cloud of dust as he turned off Union Church Road onto a small dirt road. He continued another quarter-mile to the old barn on the proposed ranch site. An aging structure of rusted metal and rotten wood, it seemed to watch over an equally haggard and overgrown pasture like an old soldier carrying a burden of duty and honor.

Staring at the old barn from inside his car, Eddie thought to himself that he wasn't real sure why he had driven there. It just seemed the appropriate thing to do. For the last several hours, he had sat inside a stuffy Atlanta high-rise office listening to and reading legalese; maybe, he just wanted to touch something real about the land that he wanted so badly for Eagle Ranch.

He already had removed his tie during the drive back from Atlanta. Sliding into the back seat of his car now, he shed the rest of his suit and jumped into a well-worn pair of Levi's, T-shirt, flannel shirt, and tennis shoes. The midday sun had broken through the clouds by then, so he decided to leave his windbreaker in the car.

In the distance, he spotted a huge pine tree towering over its kindred in the surrounding woods. He entered the thicket by the road and made his own path through the brush toward the tree. It was old and scarred but looked strong enough to last forever. Eddie sat down at the big tree's base, and at that moment the full weight and magnitude of what he had just done fell hard across his shoulders.

Looking up through the leafy branches of the tree, he stared solemnly at the broken streams of sunlight piercing through. "God, what have I done?" he said, sighing. He fought back a wave of emotion that started from his chest and moved up to his throat. It was an intense fear of failure, and it overwhelmed him.

"What have I done?" he repeated to himself. He shook his head in tired resignation. All at once, as if in answer to his own question, his anxiety left him and his whole body relaxed. Strangely, he felt a satisfying peace settle in. The feeling enveloped him like a blanket as Eddie rested back on the base of the tree.

Then, slowly, he squatted back onto his feet, grabbing the tree trunk behind him with his arms and hands for support. He pushed down on the thick trunk, inch by inch, until he was standing straight up. He wasn't dreaming. His head was as clear and fresh as a Sunday morning. But never in his life had he felt as close to God as he did at that very moment.

The sun shone down brighter as he moved away from the tree, and the warmth felt good. Moving deliberately across the land, Eddie walked the acres that he knew right then would someday be Eagle Ranch. No one could have convinced him otherwise. In silent understanding, Eddie walked from one end of the land to the other, trying to imagine what Eagle Ranch would look like someday.

Before the afternoon sun had shifted toward evening, Eddie returned to his car and drove the few miles back to the House of Grace. That night, as he retired to bed, he could hardly wait for morning — Day One of the next 120 days.

✛ ✛ ✛

After a week of little progress, Eddie finally mustered the courage to phone Bluestein and the Tarkenton Group about his signing of the contract. As he had expected, the news was not received favorably. Bluestein seemed concerned that Eddie had not informed them first.

"Marvin, I think when you see the land, you'll feel better about it. It's right in the middle of an area that's desperate for a boys' home and in a community that's conducive to raising the operational funds for the ranch."

"What's the cost?"

Eddie tensed for a second before answering. "It's part of a real-estate trust, and they're asking $144,000. Marvin, it's a great price, mainly because of a radio tower that's being built near the property. But here's the thing: The bank is requiring cash up front to settle an estate. No one will lend me the money — for obvious reasons — so I've got to raise the entire sum by August 18th."

"Eddie, I don't think Fran's going to like those terms."

Eddie knew it wasn't really the terms or the money that bothered Bluestein. It was Eddie's own business judgment that was in question.

A few days later, Bluestein called with the Tarkenton Group's decision. "Eddie, after careful consideration, we feel that it's best for us not to become involved at this time. We may at some later date, but not right now." Bluestein sounded genuinely sorry, but business was business.

As Eddie hung up the phone, he couldn't help but second-guess himself one more time. Even after turning down the Carter's Lake site, he had harbored the security that the Tarkenton Group probably would still come through with a large donation. For all intents and purposes, he had effectively closed the door on a very high hope. He would still raise the money for the ranch. But, oh my Lord, he thought. This is really going to be hard now.

Chapter Twenty-Six

Before the end of his first year at Buford Middle School, Rodney had been shifted into a special-learning class. His teachers had moved him there as much to isolate the other students from Rodney's disruptive behavior as for his own good. Rodney also was seeing two counselors, one at his school and the other at a professional office park in nearby downtown Lawrenceville. His secret thoughts of suicide had finally surfaced during a session with his school counselor, who in turn decided to refer him to a child psychologist.

Sally had flown into a near-panic attack over the news of Rodney's depression. Her boyfriend had gone through the roof, too; but Wayne's biggest concern was that the money for the new counselor would come from their own pockets. Wayne didn't put much stock in pseudo-doctors with fancy titles. He already had had it out with the school counselor who repeatedly threatened to report his intensifying efforts to discipline Rodney to the proper authorities. Wayne was furious with "the system." Who were these people to think they could tell him what to do in his own home?

But under Sally's insistence, Wayne had complied. He simply had found other ways to punish Rodney — like humiliating the boy in front of his friends. One of the most effective had involved the tall oak tree that stood to the left of the entrance to their trailer park. After Rodney had been sent home on two different occasions in one week for fighting, Wayne had ordered him to hug his arms around the tree and remain there until dark. Rodney's mischievous peers seemed to have benefited the most from the punishment. As if flocking to a public stockade, they had gathered around him gawking and laughing in amusement. A few boys had perched themselves on a nearby hill, tossing small rocks at Rodney's back and running into the woods each time one connected. Rodney knew who they were, though, and he had evened the score in a big fight the next day at school. The fights and Wayne's repercussive lessons in discipline became an endless cycle.

Rodney was bored with his young life. His only thrills seemed to be a good fight or, oddly enough, his third-period science class. Of his three special-education teachers, Rodney liked Mrs. Hampton and her science lessons the best. She shunned the typical boring lectures and slide shows for hands-on instruction. In Mrs. Hampton's class, Rodney could look at whole new worlds under a microscope, build ant colonies, or hunt for earthworms in the mud. Lately, he was fascinated with her lessons on caterpillars, cocoons, and metamorphoses. Rodney could hardly wait to view the progress each day of the tiny pupa attached to a small twig inside a glass box that was kept on a long foldaway table at the back of Mrs. Hampton's classroom. The tedious spinning of the green, silk-like web was intriguing to Rodney, and he still found it hard to believe that the little creature would eventually transform into a colorful butterfly.

One day after classes, toward the end of Buford Middle School's spring quarter, Rodney slipped into Mrs. Hampton's empty classroom to spy on the cocoon all to himself. The cocoon was now completely spun, and Mrs. Hampton had said that the metamorphosis would take place any day now. Oh, how he hoped to witness it in person! That morning in class, looking through and around the peering heads of his classmates, Rodney had noticed a slight movement inside the cocoon like a tiny heartbeat. Now, after opening the blinds nearby to let in the afternoon sun, he reveled in the chance to get a closer and unimpeded look at the strange object. His forehead pressed against the glass case and he watched. It was only a few minutes before he realized something was different.

Slowly revolving the heavy case around on the table, he noticed that the worm-like creature had torn through the back side of its silky prison. It was squirming furiously in an attempt to break free from its sticky confines. Rodney's heart raced, and he settled back on his stool to wait for the grand event that surely would unfold before his very eyes. A half-hour later, however, the creature still struggled. Rodney could wait no longer. He decided to hasten the little thing's evolution before the time got too late. He didn't want another whipping from Wayne for holding up supper.

After checking the outside hallway to ensure the coast was clear, Rodney returned to the back of the classroom and perched himself up on the table where the glass case sat. Peering down, he nervously watched as his fingers pried open and removed the glass lid. Then, with a stubby half-sharpened pencil that he found under a desk close by, he began poking around the edges of the cocoon, careful not to break the twig or harm the creature inside. A few minutes later, he had ripped through the entire cocoon from one end to the other. Rodney sat back again and watched. The creature was now totally exposed. All it had to do, Rodney figured, was fall out of the cocoon. But it did nothing, simply remaining within its shredded home. Frustrated, Rodney retrieved the pencil again and used it to physically pry the creature from its girth. It fluttered slightly in protest before falling to the glass floor of the case. Rodney now clearly saw the outline of the insect's two folded-back wings. It was a butterfly!

Outside the classroom and down the hall, a door slammed shut, breaking Rodney from his hypnotic spell. He quickly returned the glass lid over the top of the case and slipped himself under the table.

The clicking of what sounded like a woman's heels became louder, moving closer toward the classroom where Rodney hid. The person, probably a teacher, walked past the closed door and continued down the hallway.

Rodney jumped up from his hiding place and with one last look at the beautiful butterfly, he pulled open a window and scooted outside. Making sure no one was around first, he walked in a half-crouch toward the woods by the west wing of the school building. Then, under cover of the dense foliage, he ran and walked the two miles to the downtown diner where his mother worked. A good excuse had emerged from his head along the way. He would tell her that he missed the bus.

✛ ✛ ✛

The next morning, at the sound of the third-period bell, Rodney raced excitedly to Room 102 where his science class was held. He had hardly slept the night before, tossing and turning in anticipation over seeing the miracle butterfly again.

As he walked through the door, though, he was surprised to see that the butterfly's glass case had been removed. Mrs. Hampton sat at her desk, reviewing a stack of test papers. Hearing Rodney, she looked up, removed her glasses, and stared in curiosity.

"Well, this is a surprise, Rodney. I don't believe you've ever been the first student to set foot in here for third-period science."

"No ma'am, I'm just early. That's all."

Mrs. Hampton returned to her papers. Rodney walked toward his front-row desk, trying hard not to look back at the empty table. Sitting down, he opened his science book and pretended to read. His eyes shifted from side to side, scanning the room for the glass case. Where was it? Maybe Mrs. Hampton was hiding it so she could surprise the class with its amazing contents. He looked up at Mrs. Hampton and their eyes met. She had been watching him.

"Rodney, is something the matter?"

"No ma'am. Well, … yes ma'am. I was wondering what you did with the butterfly."

"Oh? Last time I saw our little cocoon, it was still in the pupa stage. Rodney, do you want to tell me something?"

"Huh?"

"You called it a butterfly just now. But when our class period was over yesterday, there was no butterfly in that glass case that I saw."

"Uh, well you said it was going to turn into a butterfly, Mrs. Hampton."

"Rodney, will you step outside please," she said, standing up from her desk. A few of the other special-education students had begun trickling into the room. One of the more trustworthy ones, Laura Jacobs, was asked to take names in case anyone misbehaved. Mrs. Hampton explained that she and Rodney would return in a few minutes.

Rodney followed his favorite teacher out the classroom door and down the school's long hallway to a small storage closet at the other end. Stopping in front of the closet door, she turned back toward Rodney and folded her arms across her chest.

"Rodney, after school was over yesterday, you slipped inside my classroom and played with our little cocoon, didn't you?"

"No ma'am."

"Rodney, …" she said, raising her voice and squinting her eyes.

He hung his head in the manner of any child who has been caught in a lie. How could she have known? "Yes ma'am, I did. But I was only helping it, Mrs. Hampton. I swear I was!"

"Rodney, you killed it."

"No ma'am, I didn't."

"Then Rodney, take a look at this."

Mrs. Hampton opened the closet and reached inside, pulling out the science project. On the bottom floor of the glass case lay a motionless, lifeless butterfly. Rodney's eyes immediately filled with tears.

"Mrs. Hampton, I swear," he said with a quivering voice. "I swear I didn't kill it."

"Rodney, exactly what did you do?"

"Well, I …" His voice was shaking so much that he had to pause to catch his breath. "I got me a pencil and poked around the cocoon to set it free. Mrs. Hampton, that little butterfly was working hard to get out of that thing, and I felt sorry for it."

"Rodney, let me tell you something." She kneeled down to face the boy at eye level. "What you did was to tamper with nature. In the last stage of the metamorphosis, the butterfly builds up its strength to fly. It does this by twisting, turning, and working to break free of its cocoon.

"By setting it free early, our little butterfly never had a chance. You didn't let nature take its course, so the butterfly was too weak to fly. And if it cannot fly, Rodney, then it cannot live."

Rodney dropped his head and burst into tears. Mrs. Hampton reached out to hug him, pulling his reddening face to her shoulder. The sounds of his crying and broken words were muffled against her dress. But she still understood him as he wailed repeatedly: "I didn't know, Mrs. Hampton. ... I didn't know-ow-ow."

Chapter Twenty-Seven

As if the daunting challenge of raising $144,000 were not enough, Eagle Ranch faced yet another obstacle on April 4, 1983, at a Hall County Planning Committee hearing. Eddie had been naive. After hearing so much vocal support from local and state juvenile officials, he had not really thought to consider the opinions of those in the ranch's backyard. Besides, Eagle Ranch was out in the middle of nowhere. Who would care?

In the days leading up to the planning meeting, Eddie received a warning from Loyd Strickland, who now sat on the Eagle Ranch Board of Directors along with David Salyers and several Gainesville-area supporters.

"I'm hearing a few rumblings out there in the south Hall community, Eddie, and they're not too favorable toward our Eagle Ranch project," Strickland had told him by phone. He listed some names, advising Eddie to visit them.

Eddie did, but it only served to confirm Strickland's suspicions. Eagle Ranch was drawing strong opposition from its future neighbors. An article had appeared recently in *Reader's Digest* magazine about a group of kids escaping from a youth detention center and murdering several people in their wake. Fueled by exaggeration and local gossip, the article had helped whip up fears that Eagle Ranch would be housing hardened criminals, posing a grave risk to the neighbors nearby.

On the evening of the zoning hearing, Eddie encountered a small but stalwart group of vocal opponents. About a dozen Chestnut Mountain residents had attended the meeting to demonstrate their concerns. The Eagle Ranch application for rezoning to a planned residential district was last on the agenda. The long wait only seemed to agitate the night's intensity.

"We're rural, and we want to stay that way!" one man shouted from the floor when the agenda finally turned to Eagle Ranch. Despite the late hour, few in the audience had left and several clapped their hands enthusiastically in agreement.

Another man, taking his turn at the microphone, asked, "What if this thing falls flat three or four years from now when you run out of money? Will you leave us an albatross? Or will the state come in here, take it over, and do whatever they want to with it?"

One by one, Chestnut Mountain property owners took the floor to address similar concerns and questions. A half-hour later, Eddie, accompanied by local attorney and Ranch board member Frank Armstrong, finally was given the floor for his response.

"I want to stress that Eagle Ranch will not be a place for hardened juvenile delinquents," Eddie said. His head slowly swept across the room as he spoke, attempting to look each person in the eyes. "We plan to build five very nice homes for children between the ages of six and eighteen who have been neglected, abused or orphaned. They won't be kids who are in trouble with the law. Our job will be to make sure they grow up to be responsible citizens.

"I promise you that Eagle Ranch will be an asset to Chestnut Mountain and all of Hall County. This community needs Eagle Ranch. The children of this region need Eagle Ranch … And we certainly need you. We need your support."

Eddie could tell his words did little to change the minds of most of the opposition in the meeting room. However, in a 3-2 vote, he received the go-ahead recommendation of the planning committee. Two members had abstained.

As he left the room that night, Eddie vowed to win the confidence someday of every community resident who had expressed even the slightest doubt over Eagle Ranch. For the moment, there was nothing he could do or say. He'd just have to show them.

The following day, he found a much more receptive audience in the Gainesville Kiwanis Club, an influential organization of local businessmen who met each Tuesday for a noontime luncheon. It was his first invitation to speak to any civic group in the community. He was introduced by Austin Edmondson, a respected Gainesville manufacturing executive who eventually would join the Eagle Ranch Board of Directors.

In his speech, Eddie laid out his ambitious growing list of goals. And with an air of confidence that continued to strengthen within him, he mentioned the thousands of dollars in contributions — almost as an aside — that would have to be raised for it all to happen. As he heard himself talk, Eddie briefly thought how impossible, even ridiculous, his plan sounded when described out loud. Judging by the faces of those in the audience, he perceived that most of them were thinking along the same lines.

"Gentlemen, I realize that what I am proposing is a miracle." A few of the murmurs in the Holiday Inn meeting room fell silent as Eddie raised his voice a notch. "But I have come here to Hall County to start a boys' home, and there is going to be a boys' home built here.

"And when it happens, it won't be because of Eddie Staub. It will be because of Jesus Christ."

A few seconds passed without a sound. Eddie continued to stand boldly at the lectern, allowing his message to sink in. Finally, from the back of the room, someone started to clap. Then one by one, each member of the club began putting his hands together until the entire room resounded loudly in an unusually long display of support.

Eddie Staub may not have convinced everyone present in the banquet room that day that Eagle Ranch had even a snowball's chance. But something more important was happening. He was winning over hearts.

✢ ✢ ✢

The Times, Opinion Page
Gainesville, Georgia
May 12, 1983

The Refreshing Dream

A man named Eddie Staub wants to build a 180-acre ranch in this community for forty abused, abandoned, and orphaned boys between the ages of six and eighteen. He has no money. Only recently, he also had no land and no "name" backers of his project. He says he is led of God in this venture.

In this belated spring season, Staub's dream is like a breath of fresh air. Too few pursue impossible dreams of selfless service with intense commitment to succeed.

As people hear of his project, they want to be a part of it. The land is available if $144,000 can be raised by August. The fund is small but building, and he now has some substantial "name" trustees.

We have the feeling this is no ordinary project. It certainly is guided by no ordinary leader.

Ted Oglesby, associate editor of the daily newspaper in Gainesville, wrote the first media story about the Eagle Ranch mission in the May 10, 1983, edition of *The Times*. The article was followed days later by an editorial praising the project as a "refreshing dream." Soon afterward, Post Office Box 1577 in Gainesville — the address set up for Eagle Ranch donations — began to get crowded. Checks ranging from $10 to $1,000 started to pack the postal box as the story of Eddie's impossible deadline captured the imagination of the community. By the end of May, forty-eight days into the race to August, Eagle Ranch had collected an astounding $30,000. Eddie and his board of directors, which had now grown to nearly ten members with a mix of Gainesville and Atlanta executives, were elated.

The local media attention also seemed to swing the tide of public support to the side of the ranch. When it came time for the Hall County Commission to review the ranch's rezoning request, the application passed unanimously. A few people had shown up to demonstrate their disapproval, but the opposition was little compared to that in the earlier planning-committee hearing. Eagle Ranch was on a roll.

✢ ✢ ✢

As was becoming a habit, Eagle Ranch continued to find help and inspiration from the most unlikely of sources. A few days after the commission vote, Eddie was driving along LaVista Road in northeast Atlanta to call on a potential donor when he had allowed his mind to wander too much off the road. By the time he reaffixed his attention, it was too late. The front bumper of his Toyota scraped into the back end of the car ahead of him. Bouncing from his car in a slight panic, Eddie rushed ahead to check on the other car's passengers. A woman, the car's only occupant, stepped out, shaking her head. She was fine, though her car's fender was not. More embarrassed than anything else he felt, Eddie apologized profusely before exchanging phone numbers with the driver, a talented Atlanta photojournalist named Nancy Dawe. Then, on a whim, he handed her some material about Eagle Ranch. What did he have to lose except maybe his license? Two days later, she called Eddie's phone number — but not to discuss his driving or her dented fender.

"Mr. Staub, I read over the material that you gave me after our little accident, and I must say that I'm fascinated by what you want to do," she had said. "Do you have any photographers to capture the beginnings of Eagle Ranch?"

When he told her he didn't, she volunteered her services — for free. Eddie accepted graciously.

On another occasion that spring, Loyd Strickland had put Eddie in touch with the retiring treasurer of the Genuine Parts Company in Atlanta. John B. Ellis, who served on the board of Strickland's foundation, was considered by many to be one of the brightest financial minds in the country. Strickland asked Ellis, as a favor, to review the proposed budget and capital building program for Eagle Ranch. The meeting took place on June 9 in Ellis' Atlanta office with two months to go and just under $100,000 left to raise before the clock struck twelve on the Bank South deadline.

After several minutes of study, the financial man looked up grimly from the papers that Eddie had given him, sighed, and shook his head. Speaking without a trace of emotion, he laid it on the line. "Eddie, I'm going to tell you something. What you're wanting to do is humanly impossible." He paused a second or two, then continued, "But then, I'm not taking into account what God can do."

Without hesitation, Eddie had popped out of his chair enthusiastically. "Thank you, Mr. Ellis. What you've just told me is very encouraging."

Ellis cocked his head slightly. He was confused.

"What you've just told me," Eddie said, "confirms something that I've felt all along. I've just never heard anyone else say it until now.

"The fund-raising deadline and all these plans for Eagle Ranch — none of it can happen except through God's hand," Eddie said. He shook Ellis' hand with genuine gratitude before bounding out the door in high spirits.

Several minutes after Eddie was gone, Ellis remained glued at his desk, still intrigued.

✢ ✢ ✢

Loyd Strickland sat in his office, reading a copy of *The Times*. The newspaper had been folded neatly into a quarter section. On the front, a troubling headline glared back at him.

The Times, Local Section

Gainesville, Georgia

July 28, 1983

Boys' Home Fund Short Of Goal

A home for neglected boys is three weeks and $40,500 short of a crucial crossroads.

That is the time and amount left for Eddie Staub to raise the necessary $144,000 to buy the property on which a ranch for homeless and neglected boys is to be developed.

Staub told *The Times* this week that he has raised $103,500 thus far and needs another $40,500 before the option to buy the property expires in three weeks.

He doesn't know where it is coming from, but then he says he hasn't known where any of the money raised so far would have come from. The whole venture has been one of faith, he says.

The news was no surprise; Eddie was keeping Strickland well-informed at their weekly board meetings. But seeing the figures reported so starkly in black and white was like a splash of cold water in his face.

Eddie was setting himself up — along with the whole community — for a major letdown. "Everything's going great. We are going to make our deadline," Eddie kept telling the board. His faith was strong, but his experience in such matters was not. Strickland had been around fund-raising long enough to know that the hardest money to raise is the last ten to fifteen percent of a goal. Eagle Ranch wasn't even that close.

Strickland picked up the phone and dialed his good friend and fellow Eagle Ranch board member Richard Shockley at Gainesville's First National Bank. Shockley served the respected financial institution — the region's largest independent — as its executive vice president.

"Richard, this is Loyd Strickland."

"How are you, my friend?"

"Right now, a little concerned. ... We're coming down to the wire on this deadline for the Eagle Ranch property, aren't we?"

"We sure are, Loyd. Eddie seems to think there's no problem, but I wonder."

"Me, too. I certainly don't want to see him fail. Not after all that he's been through."

On the other end, Shockley sat and waited, the phone cradled between his chin and shoulder. Strickland obviously was leading up to something.

"Richard, what would you think about you, me and some of the other board members setting up a blank note at the bank on behalf of Eagle Ranch? At the end of three weeks, however short we are on the money, we'll just type the necessary amount on the note. Eddie doesn't have to ever know — we can send the money anonymously."

"You can count me in, Loyd. And I agree — we can't allow Eddie and the ranch to fail now. He's been an inspiration to this whole community."

"I'll call some of the other board members."

"And I'll get the papers ready. Thanks, Loyd, for thinking of this."

Strickland hung up the phone and rocked back in his wingback leather office chair. He crossed his hands over his chest and stared up at the ceiling. Despite a difference of three decades in their ages, Eddie Staub had truly become a close friend. Strickland curved his mouth into a thin smile as he recalled the first time Eddie had walked through his office door. This tall, fresh-faced kid comes walking in here with nothing but a big idea and a lot of faith. But there was something instantly trustworthy and magnetic about him. He was pure. He was genuine. Strickland could tell right off.

They had come a long way together — he and "Staub," as Strickland liked to call his young friend — in only a short time. And he'd give anything to see him make this fund-raising deadline all on his own and without the artificial help of a secret bank note. What a testament of faith it would be for this community. What a great thing for the region's neglected kids who need a place to heal. But most of all, Strickland had to admit, he simply wanted to see the look on ol' Staub's face when that last dollar rolled in!

✦ ✦ ✦

As the clock wound down on the Chestnut Mountain property, Eagle Ranch received a major break. The Atlanta media finally picked up the story. First, Wes Sarginson, the anchor of WSB-TV's Channel 2 News, filed a moving account of Eagle Ranch's uphill battle to meet a fast-approaching deadline. A media avalanche followed with *The Atlanta Journal-Constitution* and numerous newspapers across the state that picked up the story on the Associated Press wire.

The donations, which had been slowing down through July, instantly began to pick back up. The media exposure also helped boost Eddie's credibility on his donor visits, particularly in the metro-Atlanta area. During one meeting with an Atlanta firm, he walked out the door with $12,000 in less than an hour. Eddie's name and face were becoming well-known throughout the Atlanta and Northeast Georgia region.

Eddie had never doubted that the money for Eagle Ranch would be raised in time. Still, the majority of the checks received in the mail were for less than $500, and with three days to go, Eagle Ranch was short by $7,500. He was going to need one last big push.

During the final week, Eddie spent his daytime hours making personal donor visits and his nights calling on the telephone. The Gainesville law firm of Telford, Stewart & Stewart, which had a toll-free Atlanta line, allowed him to make his calls there in the evening. On the night of August 15, he sat down at a secretary's desk in the firm's quiet, dimly lighted offices to begin another round of telephoning. He looked through a stack of phone messages collected earlier in the day from his automatic message-recording machine — a very helpful device since being donated to the ranch a few weeks earlier. One of his calls that day had been from a man named Elvin Price, who lived in Lawrenceville, county seat for the neighboring county of Gwinnett. The name was not familiar — but few were — and Eddie expected nothing unusual as he dialed the ten numbers on his call-back sheet.

"Hello?"

"Could I speak to Elvin Price, please?"

"Speaking."

"Mr. Price, this is Eddie Staub. I had a message that you called."

"Oh yeah, you're the one who's starting that boys' ranch. Thank you for returning my call."

"Sure."

"I read about you in the Atlanta papers, and I'm quite taken by your cause. I'd like to help out. Through my business — I'm the owner of Atlanta Attachment in Lawrenceville where we make various machine parts — I have a company pickup truck and a van that I thought might be useful to you."

Eddie hesitated before answering. He had received so many offers for in-kind donations, which he genuinely appreciated. But what he really needed, with time running so short, was to make some more headway on his fund-raising goal. "Yes sir, we certainly could use those things. Thank you."

"Great. Just send someone out here tomorrow. I'll sign the titles over to your ranch and you can drive them both straight off my lot. They're in great shape. You'll be pleased."

"Thank you, Mr. Price. But can I wait until next week? I'm real busy right now raising the rest of the money for our land."

"Oh, I thought you might have had that by now. How much are you short?"

"About seventy-five hundred."

"Okay, tell you what. You come visit me tomorrow, and you can drive away from here with the van, the truck, *and* a check for seventy-five hundred dollars."

"Sir?"

"I said I'll give you the check for the rest of what you need for the land. Just come by tomorrow. Now hold on and I'll give you the directions …"

✢ ✢ ✢

And just like that, Staub pulled it off, Loyd Strickland thought to himself. One phone call and he pulls off the miracle of the year — $144,000 in 120 days. Unbelievable. Absolutely unbelievable!

It had been a full twenty-four hours since Eddie called Strickland with the news. At first, Strickland had been skeptical. But then Eddie had called again that morning to confirm it. The check was collected and deposited in the bank. And just like that, Eagle Ranch was born — with only two days to spare.

Leaning back in his easy chair in the den of his home, Strickland pondered whether to wait until morning to call his good friend Richard Shockley of First National Bank. Nah … he'll be upset if he hears it second hand.

Holding a Gainesville phone book in his lap, he reached over to the phone beside him and punched out the touch-tone numbers for the Shockley residence. Shockley picked up the receiver immediately after the first ring.

"Richard?" Loyd asked to make sure, folding up the phone book in his lap and placing it back on the table beside him.

"Yes it is."

"How are you? This is Loyd Strickland."

"Loyd, how are you doing?"

"Great. Listen, sorry to bother you at this late hour, but have you prepared that note to pay off the land for Eagle Ranch?"

"Sure have, Loyd. It's sitting in my desk drawer at the office."

"Well then, I want you to do me a favor."

"What's that?"

"First thing tomorrow, I want you to pull out a pair of your sharpest scissors and slice that baby into a wastebasket-full of confetti. Our friend, Mr. Staub, has pulled it off!"

"Really? We made our goal?"

"You bet ya. Some gentleman from Lawrenceville paid off the remaining seventy-five hundred just this morning. How 'bout that?"

"That's wonderful, Loyd. Absolutely wonderful."

"It's more than that, Richard. It's a miracle. A miracle from God. This Eagle Ranch is going to be the most wonderful thing that ever happened for the needy children of this area, and we've been blessed to have been a part of it. You remember I told you so."

"Loyd, I don't doubt you a bit."

"Praise God, Richard. Praise God!"

"Amen, sir. Amen!"

EAGLE RANCH

Chapter Twenty-Eight

June 1984

Summer was settling in like a warm, musty blanket over Gainesville, and several of the local businessmen attending the regular Tuesday meeting of the local Kiwanis Club had left their coats back at the office. The rules for business attire, even among the community's bankers and lawyers, tended to relax each year when the thermometer crept into the nineties. At the head table sat a young man whose face was well-known to the Kiwanians streaming into the banquet room of the Holiday Inn. If any of the members missed his speech from the year before, they easily recognized his face from television and newspapers. Eddie Staub and Eagle Ranch shared something close to celebrity status in the wake of their inspiring success story. CNN News, whose international cable-television station was based in nearby Atlanta, had done one story touting the ranch as the "miracle on Chestnut Mountain."

Eddie had been invited back to the Gainesville Kiwanis Club to update its members. Their interest was genuine and much more than simply needing a good speaker for the weekly program, for the club had donated $20,000 toward ranch construction.

Following the usual club protocol of announcements and general business, Eddie took over the lectern to address his audience. There were no butterflies like the last time he spoke. So many of the faces were familiar to him now. He felt at home.

Eddie began his comments with a report on the recent opening of the Dr. John W. Jacobs Sr. administration building, which had been named after the father of one of the club members. The first physical structure on the Chestnut Mountain acreage, the 2,000-square-foot building would serve initially as Eddie's home and office. He joked that it was a big improvement over his office inside the old barn on the property. There, he had used four concrete bags as a desk and a donated Princess phone to conduct his business.

A dam also was under construction for the lake, and a groundbreaking for the first boys' home would be held in about a month — as soon as the entire amount of money needed for construction was raised. That was a rule that Eddie had adopted in the past year. No construction at the ranch would ever be started without the necessary funds in the bank. This debt-free philosophy had been formed unwittingly during Eddie's race to meet the land-purchase requirements. It only made sense to follow the same approach for the rest of the ranch plans; and besides, the business community loved it. Every penny of donations would go directly to the ranch, not to pay interest on a loan.

Since raising the money for the land, Eddie also had been busy planning the ranch's operational strategy. He explained to the club how the boys would be introduced to life on a farm, taking care of horses and cows while developing a strong work ethic. Amid this peaceful setting, Eddie and the houseparents whom he'd eventually hire would focus on giving troubled boys a second chance at a better life.

As he closed his remarks, Eddie recapped his fund-raising efforts, explaining how most donations to the ranch had been in small amounts of less than $1,000 per gift. It clearly demonstrated the grass-roots community support that had continued to grow over the past year.

"Gentlemen," Eddie said, pausing to sip from a glass of watered-down tea. "When I came to speak to this club a year ago, I told you that I was going to start a children's home in Hall County. And that when it was built, it wouldn't be because of me, but because of Jesus Christ. Since then, we have raised over $350,000. Look what God has done."

The room was quiet for several seconds as the room full of business men and women seemed to hang on the speaker's closing comment. Eddie felt his point sinking in — that all that had transpired at Eagle Ranch was so much bigger than what Eddie could ever have hoped to accomplish on his own.

"That was quite a sermon!" said John Jacobs Jr., son of the administration building's namesake, after the meeting was over.

Eddie shook the man's hand and thanked him. He hadn't really meant to preach to the gathering, but in a way, Mr. Jacobs was right. Eagle Ranch was more than just a future home for needy children. It was living, breathing proof of the grace and power of God.

✛ ✛ ✛

Eddie hired Eagle Ranch's first full-time employee, an administrative secretary, in July of that summer. Though he had never met her, Jean Parks had attended his same high school back in Alabama. Jean, five years younger than Eddie, was now married to a Gainesville native, Lee Parks, who had recently graduated from law school at the University of Georgia.

Eagle Ranch was more than a dream now, but its first employee found it a lonely place to work. A crudely cut dirt road led to an office isolated in the middle of 900 acres of dense woods and unfenced pasture. With Eddie on the road most days, Jean turned on a television just to break the stillness. Nevertheless, she found comfort in knowing that she was part of a noble cause and that the voices of little boys would soon replace the silence.

At night, well after Jean had left for the day, the administration office turned into a home. Since moving to Gainesville, Eddie had hopscotched from one temporary shelter to the next, all thanks to the generosity of Gainesville's caring community. After Eddie had left the House of Grace, a local doctor, Roger Owens, had arranged for him to live with his mother. A few weeks later, Harold and Sandra Law, another pair of saviors, offered the basement apartment in their home for free. Eddie stayed there for about a month until moving into a motel room at the Gainesville Day's Inn, compliments of the general manager and owner, Durwood Pennington and Charlie Thurmond. His remaining hobo days were spent only a few miles from the ranch property, at Loyd Strickland's rustic executive cabin-office on the grounds behind the Crystal Farms hatchery in Chestnut Mountain, until finally the administration building was completed.

Now, in addition to more permanent quarters, Eddie even had a roommate — Connor, a shaggy-haired golden retriever given to him by two close supporters, Bob and Nell Watt of Atlanta. Connor would become one of Eddie's best friends. Upon returning to the lonely administration building late each evening, Eddie took great comfort in seeing the dog's friendly, faithful eyes reflecting the headlight beams of his car as he pulled up to the front porch. Connor helped the place feel like home. And on Eddie's first night there, as he placed his head on his pillow in the back bedroom, he truly felt he had come to the end of a very long journey.

✢ ✢ ✢

Throughout the course of his fund-raising travels, speeches at civic clubs, and hours of manual labor spent clearing the undeveloped ranch grounds, Eddie had filled the time in between planning a program for the boys. He was relying heavily on his experience at Big Oak and observations of other boys' homes across the Southeast. Despite his preparedness, a dramatic and unexpected turn in the shape and focus of Eagle Ranch took place only a few months before the first boys' home was to be completed. The revelation unfolded the day Eddie met the man who would be his second hire.

Bruce Burch was working at the Village of St. Joseph, a residential treatment center in Atlanta for troubled children and adolescents, when he first heard of Eddie Staub and Eagle Ranch. His father, a retired industrial engineer, told him about the two after watching a news feature on television. Aware of his son's restlessness at St. Joseph's after nine years, he thought Eagle Ranch possibly might be the challenge that Bruce had been seeking.

Eddie, in turn, found out about Bruce from a friend, Diane Huey, whom he had met while attending Holy Cross Church in Atlanta. Diane knew Bruce was looking for an opportunity like Eagle Ranch, and she thought Eddie might be interested. It was almost as if Eddie was expecting the call when Bruce first phoned the ranch. Their paths seemed so destined to cross.

Their first meeting took place at the ranch property, where Eddie pretended his Toyota was really a Jeep as he chauffeured Bruce on a bumpy tour of the grounds.

"I'm impressed. You've sure got vision if you can see the makings of anything this far out in the middle of nowhere," Bruce said, his voice jiggling with every up and down contour of the makeshift roadway.

"Well, let's just say I've still got a long way to go before it all comes together," Eddie answered, smiling. "But we already have our state license and we're talking to DFACS (Department of Family and Children's Services) about scheduling the first boys to come here in a few months — just as soon as we finish building the house and hire the houseparents."

Though he kept his thoughts to himself, Bruce already liked what he saw. Throughout a long career in child care, he had longed for the opportunity to co-start an operation like Eagle Ranch.

Eddie stopped the car and pointed to the dam construction where a lake was being formed. Land on the other side of the water, he explained, would make a nice site for a chapel someday. Bruce nodded in agreement, then chuckled — all he could see was a lot of dirt, a deep hole, and a bunch of skinny pine trees.

"Are you sure you're not overqualified for the ranch?" Eddie asked.

In addition to his nine years of experience, Bruce held a master's degree in community counseling from the Psychological Studies Institute at Georgia State University.

"Well, that brings up a point that I'd like to talk to you about," Bruce said.

Eddie twisted the ignition key to the left and his car went silent. He turned halfway in his seat to listen.

"The program here that you have described briefly to me is a good one, I think. But it's missing something. What happens to the kids after they leave here?"

Eddie cocked his head. Bruce was leading up to something.

"I've worked with a lot of kids who have been bounced around from one placement to another. After a while, they learn to 'play the game,' so to speak. As long as they cover up all their problems, all the junk inside them, then everything rocks along pretty smoothly. No hassles from their caregivers. No spankings by their teachers. They become perfect little angels. Then, one day it's time to leave for the real world, and boom — it all falls apart.

"It's sad, but a lot of hurting children out there are falling through the cracks because no one is addressing their real issues. Most caregivers can handle the child's physical needs well enough … clothes, food on the table … But that's not enough. Their emotional needs are just as, if not more, critical."

Eddie listened intently. Bruce obviously was impassioned in his views, but he also made good sense. It was a perspective that Eddie, until that moment, had not explored.

"Do you think we could handle both needs here?"

"It would be a challenge, but yes I do. As you have described it to me, Eagle Ranch — like most group home operations — would be a custodial-type program. We could develop a therapeutic one … a program that addresses all the issues that brought these kids here in the first place. Then, we would deal with each problem head-on with individual, group and family counseling. I really believe you've got to heal the pain of their past before the kids can begin to look to the future."

There was a fire in the eyes of this wise, athletic-looking man who sat beside him, and Eddie found himself getting excited. Deep in the rural backwoods of Chestnut Mountain, Eagle Ranch had the opportunity to blaze a bold new path in child care. It would transcend the custodial models of the past and work to mold troubled boys from the inside out with sensitive but aggressive counseling. Eddie immediately knew he had stumbled onto a whole new course. And counselor Bruce Burch was just the person to help him see it through.

Chapter Twenty-Nine

April 1985

By the time the first boys were referred to Eagle Ranch in the spring of 1985, the beginnings of a therapeutic program were taking shape. Together, Eddie and Bruce had begun to design a model boys' home joining their own ideas with the best of tried and true child-care practices at children's homes across the Southeast.

To create an atmosphere resembling, as closely as possible, an actual family setting, Eddie insisted that no home should take on more than eight children — as opposed to the typical ten kids per home at most facilities. Also, one houseparent couple would be assigned to each home on a long-term basis. Eddie did not want the children being passed from one parent "shift" to the other. These kids, for the first time in their lives, deserved to have a little stability, from which a strong foundation could begin to be rooted.

Although he wanted to open the doors of Eagle Ranch to as many boys as possible, Eddie vowed not to become a warehouse. He strongly believed that any more than forty to fifty children and the ranch would begin to take on the character and feel of an institution. He also sought to build only the highest-quality homes and facilities for the boys of Eagle Ranch. Eddie would see to it that they received the best of everything — from food, clothing, and housing to an abundance of love and attention.

Still, the boys of Eagle Ranch would not be "normal" boys. They would come with broken hearts, some with broken bodies from a life of physical abuse. They would require a much different upbringing that went above and beyond the typical family setting. Discipline, strict discipline, would be necessary — but in a fashion that most of the kids would never have experienced before. For while Eddie, as a future parent, might spank his own child, he understood the likely futility of such punishment with the boys who would live at Eagle Ranch. To them, a spanking would only hurt, not help. Indeed, some of the boys probably would have experienced such horrible beatings that they would be jaded to any form of physical discipline. With this understanding, Eddie and Bruce designed a reward system based on specific accomplishments. The program would be played out in terms that a youth would understand and even find to be fun.

Every boy would enter the ranch as a "crow" — the bottom rung of life at Eagle Ranch. By working hard and studying hard, the crow could graduate to "hawk," earning special privileges such as staying up an hour later on Saturday night or getting a special snack during the day. Next in line was "falcon," and at the top of the level system — the rung to which all the boys should aspire — would be the "eagle."

Christian life would be modeled and taught in every home with no one denomination ever stressed over another. Spiritual development, Eddie believed, was the key to instilling rock-solid morals for a child's future.

Completing the circle in the Eagle Ranch program was the counseling approach that had taken shape in the final hour. Bruce Burch would conduct regular counseling sessions with each child in an attempt to discover the root cause of a problem and work diligently to correct it. Each boy would go through one individual session and one group session every week. Twice a month, counseling sessions would be held with the child and his parents. Bruce also would provide training for the houseparents to help them cope better with each child.

Eddie had borrowed ideas and innovated a few of his own to assemble what he hoped would be an evolving program addressing four critical development areas in any child: physical, emotional, intellectual, and spiritual growth. By implementing the model within the simulated nest of a stable family atmosphere, Eagle Ranch's overriding goal would be to reunite each child with his own natural parents — the boys would even be required to leave the ranch bimonthly for visits back home. There surely would be incidences in which family reconciliation was hopeless, and in those cases, the ranch staff would do its best to prepare each boy for the day he left the ranch. No child could hold onto Eagle Ranch forever — age eighteen or high-school graduation would be the limit — but Eddie hoped at least to impart enough love and hope along with the basic tools for success to follow each boy for the rest of his life.

After three years of hardship and struggle, the real work was about to begin. Everything seemed in place, Eddie thought. Now he hoped and prayed that all of it would really work.

✢ ✢ ✢

Tony and Trish Dittmeier seemed to fit the perfect mold for houseparents. Eddie had hoped to find capable, committed Christian couples willing to give up two to three years of their lives to raise and heal an extended family of hurting, disadvantaged boys. They had to be devoted to the Eagle Ranch cause — not simply looking for a place to which to escape.

Both husband and wife were achievers. Tony, a former Marine, was a program manager in the Federal Transit Administration. Trish was a schoolteacher with a master's in education. They had two children, a four-year-old daughter, Emily, and a six-year-old son, Andrew. Both expressed to Eddie a "call" from God to uproot their comfortable lifestyle in Tucker, Georgia, to become the first houseparents of the upstart Eagle Ranch program. On April 7, they moved into what was called the "Faith Home." (Eddie planned to name all the homes at the ranch after Christian virtues — "Faith," "Hope," "Love," and "Peace" would be the first four.)

Tony and Trish had less than a week to settle in before Eagle Ranch's first son arrived. Jerry, a ten-year-old stick of dynamite, would prove to be a formidable initiation. Diagnosed as having a behavioral disorder, the boy had been placed unsuccessfully in several foster homes and special schools. Boys with such serious psychological problems were not the ideal applicants at Eagle Ranch, because its program was best designed to help kids on the "front end" of their problems. But Eddie couldn't say no to this referral from Fulton County; he was anxious to get his program started and begin building a track record.

The next few boys came from all walks of life, and Eddie eventually realized there was no sense looking for the "perfect" Eagle Ranch child. Some, like six-year-old Zack, were from lower-income homes; but then there was Bobby, who grew up in a wealthy family, one showering him with toys, money, and trips — virtually everything that a kid could want, except for love. Bobby's parents had neglected him for years, leaving him at home for several weeks at a time with different nannies while traveling across the world. When the couple divorced a year before he came to the ranch, Bobby's world was thrown even deeper into isolation. At age fourteen, he had become an unruly rebel constantly up for suspension at school. A counselor at his private school had suggested Eagle Ranch, and Bobby reluctantly agreed to the living arrangements, expecting to find another lavish summer camp like so many before. Eagle Ranch was far from it, and it threw him into a temper tantrum after only his second night in the Faith Home. He was unfamiliar with any family structure, and the thought of being asked to take out the garbage among other menial chores angered him. Equally taken aback were Tony and Trish, but they battened down the hatches and dug in for the duration. They told themselves over and over: "We'll get through this. We'll weather Jerry. We'll weather Bobby.

And with God's help, we'll handle all the rest who come through our door. No one ever promised us it would be easy."

Within two months, the Dittmeier home was almost full. In addition to their own two children, they had collected a band of six young pirates. Technically, there was room for one or two more, but Eddie wondered if it would be possible to handle them. The Faith Home was close to coming apart. After such a fast start, he already was ready for life at Eagle Ranch to settle down a bit.

So it was with some reluctance that Eddie even agreed to meet with the fifteen-year-old boy referred by a counselor from nearby Duluth. Jacob was getting his first taste of the South after moving down from Baltimore, where he had been bounced back and forth among the extended family of his deceased parents. For now, it was his grandmother's turn to look after him, and she was close to giving up. The north-to-south change in locales had done nothing to improve her grandson's behavior. Having gone through the sixth grade three times back in Maryland, he was still cutting class and flunking every subject in school. Finally, she agreed to take the counselor's advice and attempt to send Jacob to Eagle Ranch. He needed more structure in his life, the counselor told her. Besides, it was only for a year, and Jacob could come home twice a month under this relatively new and innovative program in Chestnut Mountain, Georgia.

For Jacob, however, the first few days of Eagle Ranch were more like a prison. Used to a lackadaisical independence that came from being ignored most of his young life, Jacob suddenly was subjected to close supervision. It was a miserable existence, and twice he was caught running away from home.

"You guys will just have to keep coming after me," Jacob told Tony Dittmeier, his most recent father figure in a long string of make-believes. "I've got rabbit in my blood."

After two months, Jacob held to his word, making everyday life in the Dittmeier home a test of patience and endurance. His unruliness was beginning to interrupt the small progress made with the other boys. Finally throwing in the towel, Tony went reluctantly to

Eddie's office to discuss Jacob's removal.

"Eddie, I'm afraid we've met our first impossible kid. Jacob simply is not working out. Even worse, he's upsetting the other boys."

"I'm sorry you and Trish have had it so rough," Eddie said.

"Oh, don't apologize. I just wish there was something we could do for him. Jacob really needs help. He's so mixed up now, but he refuses to let us or Bruce try to help him. He can't deal with chores and discipline, so he thinks the only way to deal with his problems is to run away. I'm not sure how much longer we can keep him here."

Following several days of prayer and deliberation, Eddie finally decided to force a resolution. It would take place on a hot, late Saturday morning in mid-July. Calling Jacob into his office, he went straight to the point.

"Tony tells me you're not keeping up with your chores. You're not studying either, and your grades at summer school are showing it. And last week, he caught you out by the highway trying to run away again. … Jacob, what are we going to do with you?"

"I don't like all these rules you got here. It's like some prison."

"Do you want to leave Eagle Ranch?"

Eddie expected an immediate "yes," but it wasn't what he heard. Looking down at the dark-stained wood floor in the administration office, Jacob merely shrugged his shoulders.

"I asked you, 'Do you want to leave Eagle Ranch?'"

"I dunno. … maybe."

"Listen, you need to make a decision. But I'll guarantee you this. If you stay here, you're going to follow the rules."

Jacob stood up from his chair without a word and shuffled his feet toward the front door.

"Not so fast," Eddie said in a stern voice. "I've got forty pine tree seedlings out back that need planting along the main road. If you're to stay at Eagle Ranch, you're going to plant all forty of them today."

Ignoring Eddie's words, Jacob continued walking until he reached the door.

"Jacob ..."

Showing no hesitation, the boy turned the door's silver handle and walked outside, never looking back. Eddie shook his head in resignation, staring at the closed door. This time, Jacob had crossed the line, and just like that it was over. Eddie winced as he sat back down at his desk, realizing he had just witnessed the ranch's first big failure.

✞ ✞ ✞

Later that afternoon, Eddie rose from the administrative paperwork scattered before him to take a break. He had worked through lunch without a bite and several more hours without leaving his chair in order to clear the pile of papers backed up on his desk. Massaging his stiff neck with one hand, he stepped outside the lobby door where the sun still glared down hard. He looked down one end of the porch and smiled at the sight of Connor, his dog, sleeping soundly within the smallest sliver of a shadow. The dog's tongue was hanging out, and he was panting involuntarily.

A few seconds later, Eddie cocked his head in curiosity at the sound of something crunching in the distance. Raising a cupped hand to his eyes to shield the falling sun on the horizon, he squinted to focus on a spot along the main road, where he saw a lone figure. It was Jacob. The boy had planted close to fifteen seedlings and was working to crack the hard-baked Georgia clay to sink one more.

"Jacob! Come here!"

The boy, a black profile against the sun from 100 yards away, took a few more stabs at the earth, then slowly started walking toward the office. Eddie could see total exhaustion in the boy's trudging stride. A few feet before he reached the porch, Eddie noticed Jacob's clothes were sopped with perspiration. Wetness also streamed down his face and neck — it was difficult to tell whether it was sweat or tears, but Eddie assumed it was a combination of both.

"Jacob, why don't you call it a day. You can plant the rest tomorrow."

"Eddie?"

"Yes?"

"Can you get me some gloves for tomorrow?"

He looked down at Jacob's hands and saw several ugly, swollen blisters. Sharp pain shot through Eddie's heart at the sight of the boy's agony. He looked Eddie in the eyes, and Eddie nodded yes. All at once, Jacob's body seemed to collapse and Eddie caught him in mid-stride. Together they held on to each other in the hot sun as Jacob began to sob with his whole body.

"Let it out, Jacob," Eddie said, straining to keep his own voice from cracking. "Just let it all out."

Chapter Thirty

Fall 1985

Eddie sat down at the head of the makeshift conference table of the Eagle Ranch administration office. Seated around him were Tony, Trish, Bruce, and Jean. With the boys back in school for the fall quarter, they were able to gather at one table for what seemed like the first time since the ranch opened. It certainly had to be the quietest moment shared together in the past six months.

"Well, guys. How's it going?" Eddie asked to open the meeting.

One by one, progress reports were given on each boy by houseparents Tony and Trish, then by Bruce, who gave an overview of his counseling sessions, while Jean, the administrative secretary, dutifully took notes. Jacob was the biggest success story to date. Bruce informed the group that the boy finally was beginning to unload some of his troubles in their sessions together.

"We're going through junk that has been locked away since he was a little fellow," Bruce said.

Trish, in her ever-ebullient manner, chimed in: "I'm just amazed at how far Jacob's come. He even pulled up his grades to two B's and a C by the end of summer school! That's pretty good considering he was on the verge of flunking everything."

"He's keeping up with all his chores now, and I haven't had to discipline him even one time in the last few weeks," Tony added. "He's a good kid. I'm just as proud of him as if he were my own son."

Bruce reported that his meetings with Jacob's grandmother were less encouraging. Citing health reasons, the woman said she couldn't keep up her bimonthly get-togethers with Jacob. They were too much of an inconvenience.

"All I can hope is that we help prepare Jacob for life on his own," Bruce said, "because I'm not very optimistic that he's going to ever get much help from his grandmother or any other relative. He really has no home other than Eagle Ranch."

Eddie continued down the list of boys, listening to updates from the different perspectives of each staff member. The discussion was followed by an interchange of possible strategies for dealing with each child. Eddie was proud of his small staff and felt fortunate that each of them had followed their hearts to the ranch. He couldn't help but remember what his father used to tell him: "Son, the key to success in any organization is to surround yourself with successful people." Dad sure would have approved, Eddie thought, smiling.

Six months definitely was too early to tell, but the Eagle Ranch concept on paper seemed to be working in practice. Eddie realized he could never expect a 100 percent success rate, but for every Jacob whose life was turned around, it sure would help him feel like all the hard work was worth it. Their jobs at Eagle Ranch truly had the potential of reaching far beyond just one boy to influence the lives of many others who crossed paths with that boy in the course of a lifetime — and generations beyond.

"Okay, everyone, I've got one more item to bring up," Eddie said. Their upbeat meeting had gone well over the scheduled hour, and everyone seemed to be enjoying the fellowship. "I wonder, Tony and Trish, if you think you could take on one more kid?"

"Hey, wait a minute," Bruce interjected. "I thought you said no more until the Hope Home is completed next spring. Things have settled down a little, but Tony and Trish are still stretched to the limit."

"We're okay, Bruce," Tony said. "What have you got, Eddie?"

"I got a call yesterday from a school counselor at a middle school in Buford. She says she's heard good things about the ranch, and there's a fourteen-year-old kid there who she thinks we might be able to help."

Eddie folded his arms behind his head and leaned back in his chair to stretch his long body. The staff focused intently on Eddie's face, waiting for the rest of the story.

"The counselor says the boy is bright ... very bright, in fact. But he has a long history of abuse by his father who passed away a few years ago. The man was killed in some sort of police chase while attempting to kidnap the boy from his ex-wife. Right now, the kid is back to living with his mother and her boyfriend in a trailer park off I-985 in Buford. The counselor told me he apparently doesn't get along with his mother's boyfriend. He gets real despondent and talks a lot about suicide."

"Is there any evidence that he's being abused now?" Trish asked.

"Not that they can tell. The boyfriend, though, evidently can go a little overboard with his discipline, but nothing real serious."

"I say that we interview him with his mother, like all the rest, and we make our decision then," Bruce said. "Tony, Trish ... are you all right with that?"

"Sure," answered Trish.

"No problem," Tony echoed.

"By the way, what's the boy's name?" Trish asked.

"Rodney, I think," Eddie answered, looking down at a few scribbled notes on a desk pad. "Yeah, that's it. Rodney Hudgins."

✛ ✛ ✛

Eagle Ranch held its first big public gathering — a picnic supper — on September 12, 1985. Loyd Strickland had generously offered his company's pavilion, located beside a beautiful pond behind the Crystal Farms plant, for the grand event. It was a celebration of the ranch and all those who had lent a hand along the way. Eddie was deeply moved to see all of his supporters together for the first time. There were dignitaries like Coach Vince Dooley, several state representatives, senators and members of the Hall County Board of Commissioners. The ranch's large number of local board members — John Cromartie Jr., Frank Armstrong, Richard Shockley, Austin Edmondson, Roger Brown, John McKibbon III, Martin Ellard, Tom Hodge, Coulter Maginnis, John Stanley, Dorothy Rucker, Bobby Strickland, and Dr. Roger Owens — had attended, as well as Eddie's good friend, David Salyers, who continued to drive up from Atlanta to attend board meetings. Other out-of-town board members included Julius Bishop, Bill Curry, Jon Kubler, Bill Stark, Richard McDevitt, and Elvin Price. Victor Gregory also made time to attend the event. How could Eddie ever repay this man for believing in him when he had no reason to? Nancy Dawe, who continued to put together a photographic record of the Eagle Ranch construction, came along with so many other supporters who had donated their time and talents. Several news media reporters attended like Wes Sarginson, Ted Oglesby and others whose stories were so critical toward building excitement for the ranch project. Close friends and advisors Bob and Nell Watt joined the crowd along with the Rev. Randy Pope, who drove up from Atlanta to give the invocation. The list went on and on. Eddie feared he might miss shaking someone's hand at the picnic or fail to adequately express his thanks for their support. He could not have accomplished anything without them.

Toward the evening's close, Eddie stood up from his picnic bench to address the gathering and provide an update on the ranch. On purpose, he didn't mention the need for operating or building funds. He had vowed long before to be low key in his money-raising efforts. God would always provide. The audience was hushed in amazement as Eddie made his report. It was hard, even for Eddie, to grasp all that had been accomplished in the past several months.

Next, he outlined the ranch's future direction with the construction of the Hope Home in the spring and two more 6,000 square-foot homes after that. A ten-acre lake would be filled soon, and the clearing was nearly completed for an athletic field and livestock pastures that would give the kids plenty of room to roam. Very soon, Eagle Ranch would be the largest children's home in Northeast Georgia.

At the end of his brief speech, the crowd clapped for a long time, punctuating the tremendous early success of Eagle Ranch. Amid the resounding applause, Eddie felt God's pleasure.

✛ ✛ ✛

Eddie walked into his office Monday morning a few minutes late for an appointment. Seated in the small lobby across from Jean Parks' desk were a woman and boy whose backs were turned slightly so that neither faced the other.

"Hello. You must be Mrs. Hudgins. I'm sorry I'm late."

The woman stood up and extended a trembling hand. "That's okay. Oh, excuse my shaking; I've been trying to quit smoking, and it's not going so well."

"And you must be Rodney?"

The boy turned around further to face the wall, saying nothing. He wore a punk-rock T-shirt of some kind, an earring in one ear, and dirty long hair that stretched across his bony shoulders.

"Okay, we'll talk later. Mrs. Hudgins, would you like to join me in my office?"

Sally rose from her seat, embarrassed, and followed Eddie to his desk. After closing his office door, he began a routine line of questioning to learn more about her son.

"My boy has been through a lot, Mr. Staub. His dad nearly killed him in a car wreck — that's where he gets that scar on his lip, and he still limps a little bit, too. What scares me the most lately is all his talk of killing his self. Sometimes, I think he really means it."

Eddie saw the hurt in Sally's face and knew right away that the woman truly loved her boy. Under the circumstances, she probably had done the best job she could to raise her son on a meager income. Eddie was touched by her concern and hoped that Eagle

Ranch could find a way to help.

"Mrs. Hudgins, our counselor will need to conduct an interview with your son before we decide whether to admit him. And then there'll be some other small details like getting his hair cut — little stuff like that if he's accepted. But that can wait for now. First, why don't I take you on a tour to help you make up your own mind?"

"Oh, I'm willing to try anything at this point. If y'all will have him, I'll let you take him."

"Well, just remember that our whole purpose is to keep families together. We'll give him a good home while he's here, but it's only temporary. And you'll get to see Rodney twice a month."

"Good."

"Okay, let's take that tour."

In the lobby, Rodney still sat with his chair turned around to face the wall. Eddie invited him to join them, but he chose to continue his small rebellion.

"Rodney, you get out of that chair right now and thank this man!"

Rodney stood slowly, then walked past both his mother and Eddie to the door and their car outside.

"It's okay, Mrs. Hudgins," Eddie said softly.

✝ ✝ ✝

A few days after his visit, Rodney was admitted into the Eagle Ranch program as its eighth boy. He moved timidly into a full Faith Home on an early Saturday morning. It took less than ten minutes to unpack the car — Rodney had only two small suitcases and a Sunday suit on a hanger. To Tony and Trish, Sally seemed uneasy and awkward as she watched her son settle in. There was a look on her face that said she wanted to stay longer but knew it was time to let Rodney get on with his new life.

The Dittmeiers felt pain and a little guilt — as they did with each new child — in seeing another mother or father turning over their son to two strangers. Sally reached out to hug her only son — the boy that she loved more than anyone and anything on earth. But Rodney ignored her, turning instead and retreating to his designated bedroom upstairs.

"We'll take good care of him, Mrs. Hudgins. We promise," Trish said, trying hard not to cry over the woman's grief.

Sally didn't seem to hear her. She stared distantly at the stairwell that led to her son's room. Rubbing her left temple, she then turned back toward Trish and Tony and smiled weakly.

"Thank you. I know you'll take care of my boy. He's really a good boy, just a little ..." Sally's words stuck in her throat, and tears began streaming down the cheeks of her face.

Trish immediately walked to her side and wrapped her arms around the woman. But Sally resisted the show of affection, pushing Trish away gently as she quickly regained her composure. She wiped away her tears with the back of one hand.

"I'll be on my way now. Thank you." Sally walked out the front door and slid into the front seat of her car. After closing the car door, she clicked open the glove compartment and rifled through the clutter for several seconds before pulling out a single cigarette. She hurriedly lighted up and took a heavy drag, which seemed to relax her for the moment. Then, turning over the ignition, she drove the car out of the driveway and onto the dusty gravel road leading toward the Eagle Ranch entrance. Once on the main highway, she accelerated well past the speed limit, quickly putting as many miles as she could between her and her son. Subconsciously, she was racing to outrun her pain.

✝ ✝ ✝

The Faith Home finally exploded — or at least it felt that way to Tony and Trish. Rodney's introduction to his new family had seemingly gone very well for the first few days. He cooperated fully in getting his hair cut, and his shyness and quiet demeanor almost lulled them into letting down their battle defenses. But Trish reacted fast when the first salvo was launched one early evening on a school night. Rodney erupted into a fight with Jacob, who shared his bedroom, and two other boys, Bobby and Jerry, who lived across the hall. Rodney had somehow picked three fights at once in a brazen effort to stake his turf. Trish jumped into the middle of the pile to pull the boys apart before realizing she was overmatched.

"Tony! ... Tony!" she screamed at the top of her lungs. Then focusing back on the boys, she pleaded for them to stop. It was no use. All four were out of control.

Jacob was the first to pull away. In the distance, he heard Tony bounding up the stairs and quickly sobered his anger. The others were not quite as attentive, and Rodney couldn't have cared less. As Tony entered the room, the fight stopped as suddenly as it had started, though Rodney was still swinging at empty air and calling for more.

"Rodney, calm down at once!" Tony bellowed. "This house is much too small for everyone not to get along, so cool it!"

Rodney stood panting for breath, his face red with anger. He stared at Tony's intimidating size and decided quickly to obey. This man probably could wallop me pretty good, he figured.

In a stern but serene voice that seemed to defuse the electricity of the moment, Tony commanded each boy to sit down on the floor and explain — starting with Jacob — what had just transpired.

"This jerk here thinks he already owns our room," Jacob spurted.

"Jacob, I asked for an explanation — not fighting words. And by the way, no matter who started this thing, there's no excuse for hitting somebody."

Jacob's eyes teared up, realizing his mistake. With one fell swoop, he had put all his hard work toward becoming a falcon into jeopardy. It truly was to have been a badge of honor and respect for him — not simply a way to watch more television or stay up later on weekend nights.

Tony heard similar stories from Bobby and Jerry, both of whom pointed the finger squarely at Rodney. By the time Rodney's turn came, he figured it was useless to defend himself. As usual, he was the outcast. It was always his fault.

"Rodney, I asked you for your side of the story."

"I ain't saying, but I'll tell you one thing. Three on one ain't fair."

"Rodney's right, boys. Three on one is not fair, and all three of you — Jacob, Bobby, Jerry — have lost television privileges for the rest of the week."

"What about him?" all three said in chorus, glaring at Rodney.

"Rodney is new here, and I think we should cut him a little slack until he gets accustomed to how we operate around here. Understood?"

"Yes sir." "Yes sir." "Yes sir," they all answered one after the other.

"Rodney, get your jacket. I think we both could use a little walk to settle down before bedtime."

Outside, neither Rodney nor Tony said a word for the first few minutes of their walk. Tony was being patient. Rodney was plain confused. He didn't understand how the system worked: Was he going to be punished or not? After a few more minutes of silence, he could bear the suspense no longer.

"I'm sorry, Tony."

"For what, Rodney?"

"For the fight."

"You started it, didn't you?"

They both stopped and Tony waited for the answer. But Rodney stared down at his feet and resumed his silence. He still feared the consequences that might come with a free admission of guilt.

Tony didn't press. Changing the subject, he pointed to the pasture that wrapped along the gravel road. "Whatta ya say we crawl under this fence and take a look at the stars?"

"Sir?"

"The stars. Out here, it gets so dark at night that you can see the entire Milky Way. Come on."

Pulling up the barbed wire carefully, Tony helped Rodney slide through the fence, then he followed behind. They walked several hundred feet to a small rise in the open field and plopped down together on their backs in the tall grass.

"What did I tell you? Have you ever seen so many stars in your whole life?"

"No sir."

They sat back and said nothing more between them until Rodney estimated it was well past his mandatory bedtime. Without moving his head, he shifted his eyes to the left to look at Tony. He was still staring skyward.

"Your mother called last night," Tony said, interrupting the peaceful stillness. "She just wanted to know how you were doing. Said you had forgotten your jacket, and she was worried you might need it pretty soon. She asked us not to tell you she had called, but I thought you ought to know."

Rodney closed his eyes and stopped watching the stars.

"She really loves you."

"Does not!" Rodney yelled back angrily with two short bursts of air.

Tony waited a few seconds for Rodney's temper to simmer back down, then turned his head in the grass to face him. "Rodney, I want you to try and forgive your mother for whatever you think she's done to you."

"You don't know how messed up she is. She's messed up my whole life."

"Maybe so, but that doesn't mean she doesn't love you or that she's not trying to make things better for you. She wouldn't have asked us to help you if that was the case."

For the next several minutes, Tony gently picked through Rodney's battered life, exploring piece after piece in search of what was wrong. He learned a little about Rodney's horrible abduction and the painful stay afterward in the hospital. Rodney also told him about his mother's boyfriend and how much he hated him as well as his mother for sinking low enough to live with him. Soon, he was talking nonstop, unlocking the secret stories of a few given-up attempts to end his life. Crying intermittently between words, he described a barren world devoid of sunshine and filled with nightmares. A whole half-hour eventually went by with Tony saying nothing, only listening. Rodney had lost himself in his own sorrow, almost forgetting the companion next to him in the cool grass.

As if waking from a dream, Rodney abruptly stopped in mid-sentence to turn and look at Tony. The boy's heart jumped and his mouth gaped open in confusion. Reflected in the eerie light of the evening, he saw Tony Dittmeier — this big, strong and masculine ex-Marine — weeping in mournful whispers.

✢ ✢ ✢

Bruce picked up where Tony had left off the following week, studying Rodney's battered emotions in their first counseling session. They had jumped into an easy, friendly conversation that seemed to be going well until Bruce focused his microscope on Rodney's relationship with his mother. The change in subject produced an angry outburst, and Bruce decided to back off for the time being. He shifted to a more positive approach.

"You've never mentioned to me what sort of activities that you like. Do you like football? Horseback riding? Fishing? What do you like?"

"Nothing, really."

"Come on, there must be something you really enjoy doing."

Rodney was still miffed. Digging in, he refused to answer. He didn't like people taking up for his mother. She didn't deserve it.

"Rodney?"

"I said nothing. I'm no good at nothing."

"Rodney, I know that's not true. Already, I can tell that you're very intelligent. You could be good at anything you wanted if you set your mind to it."

Rodney decided he would set his mind to being difficult. Bruce was irritating him. "Fightin'."

"What did you say?"

"I said, fightin'. That's what my mother's boyfriend says. He says the only thing I'm good at is fightin'."

Bruce fielded the comment and threw it back. "That's great."

Rodney's mouth hung open in surprise. "Huh?"

"I said that's great. … Someday, you're going to take on a lot of big battles, Rodney, and I'm not talking about the ones with your fists. You're going to need that fighting spirit of yours to overcome what life is going to throw at you. But in the meantime, let's concentrate on channeling that energy into something positive. You say you're a good fighter, then let's make you an even better one. I think you should go out for the wrestling team at school."

Rodney initially shook off Bruce's remark, thinking he was joking. But Bruce continued to urge him during the next several days until Rodney yielded just to get the counselor off his back. Bruce was really getting on his nerves.

His tryout at Johnson High School met with an equal amount of skepticism from peers and the faculty. All the Eagle Ranch boys were regarded with suspicion, like renegades from a foreign land. But Rodney turned out to be a surprisingly good wrestler — a fact that shocked him more than anyone. Very soon, he was expending so much energy on the mat that it left little energy for fights in the classroom. Eddie joked among his staff that Rodney had broken a personal best record — two whole weeks without a fist fight.

For several weeks, Rodney dove headlong into his new passion, showing up early every day for practice and working out with weights at every opportunity to build up his tiny frame. By the end of October, Rodney easily earned a starting position on the junior-varsity team. But his coach was so impressed that he talked to the varsity coach about entering Rodney in the lightweight class. Rodney was excited and scared at the same time. As a freshman, he was intimidated by the bigger boys on the varsity. But he continued to do well and was slotted in the second-string position behind an experienced senior in the 103-pound weight class.

Tony and Trish and the rest of Rodney's new family surprised him one night with a combination fifteenth birthday party and celebration over his making the varsity. Rodney's mother had been invited too, but, oddly, she had declined. She didn't want to spoil it for him, she told Tony.

At the party and all through the winter, Rodney was all smiles. His self-esteem elevated to a level he had never known, he felt the happiest in all his life. After one of the daily family devotionals, in which Rodney had learned how to pray for the first time, he asked for his first big favor from God. He asked to be blessed to stay at Eagle Ranch for the rest of his life.

Chapter Thirty-One

Eddie knew he was asking for trouble when he came up with the idea. But his heart won out over common sense, and he announced at a staff meeting that he and Bruce had planned a three-day trip for the five boys who remained at the ranch during the two-week Christmas break. One of the ranch benefactors had graciously offered the use of a beach house at Amelia Island off northern Florida's Atlantic coast.

"But Eddie, it's too cold to go the beach," said Trish.

"Nah, … just too cold to go swimming. The boys can still get out on the beach. They'll go nuts when they hear about it, especially Rodney. He's never been outside the state of Georgia or even seen the ocean before."

"You guys are going to have five tigers by the tails, believe me," Tony said, shaking his head in amusement. "But more power to you if y'all think you can handle it. You sure you don't need me to come along?"

"Tony! Would you leave me at home all alone with Emily and Andrew? I'd have to go, too!" Trish interjected in mock astonishment.

"Hold on a minute, guys," Eddie said, playing referee. "That's part of the reason that Bruce and I are going. We felt that you and Tony needed a little peace and quiet — some time to spend with your own family for a change. It's been a long year."

"Eddie's right," Bruce said. "You guys have been going full speed ever since April. Let Eddie and me take the heat for a while."

"Okay, twist my arm a little harder!" Trish said, her eyes twinkling as she spoke. "We'll see how good you two are at playing Mom and Dad!"

✝ ✝ ✝

The trip to Amelia Island in the Eagle Ranch minivan had been the longest eight hours that either Bruce or Eddie could ever remember. Along the way, they had been asked "how much longer?" at least a dozen times, stopped for bathroom and snack breaks at least every half-hour, and broken up three scuffles. Still, they shared the excitement of the boys. As it turned out, Rodney was not the only boy who had never seen the ocean. Jacob and little Zack also were first timers. Bruce and Eddie couldn't wait to get there and see their faces.

"How much longer?" Bruce kidded, leaning over from a back seat to nudge Eddie as they neared the Fernandina Beach exit off Interstate 95.

"All right, Bruce. I'm going to make you sit up front if you don't behave."

Another hour down the road, the non-stop yelling, laughing and teasing stopped, oddly, all at once. Eddie looked into the rear-view mirror to see what was wrong. He saw five little heads scrunched up together against the windows on the left side of the van. They had spotted the ocean.

"Eddie?" asked Zack, the youngest of the boys.

"Yes?"

"That's the ocean?"

"Yes it is."

"Well, I don't understand."

"What don't you understand, Zack?"

"Where's the other side?"

The quietness of the moment dissipated into a loud cacophony of guffaws and teasing. Even Bruce and Eddie were hard-pressed not to smile.

Around 5 p.m., the van pulled up to the beach house and all five boys catapulted from the van. It was still just light enough to see the massive, glistening object of their wonderment. Bruce joined the boys down by the surf to keep them in check, while Eddie stayed behind to unpack the van. Tony was right. They sure had five uncaged tigers on their hands. And with each passing hour, their excitement seemed to escalate until two days later, on Saturday night, it finally got them into trouble.

Earlier that day, Jacob and Rodney met two girls on the beach. In no time, both boys knew deep down in their hearts that they were in love. The young courtships had gone on for most of the day until Eddie and Bruce called the boys inside the villa for a fresh homemade seafood dinner of shrimp and fish. Following the meal and an agonizing half-hour of cleaning dishes, Jacob and Rodney returned immediately to the beach to join their two new loves.

"Hey guys!" Bruce yelled as they ran out the door. "Don't forget the curfew!"

An 8 p.m. curfew had been set down by Bruce and Eddie, but this night it would be forgotten. Young Romeo and Casanova suffered a temporary loss of memory during a long moonlit walk in the surf. They were having the times of their lives.

Back at the villa, Eddie became slightly worried when the boys failed to return after eight. An hour later, he and Bruce were in a near panic, fearing the worst. They didn't have to remind each other that neither boy knew how to swim. Heading outside, Bruce and Eddie briefly walked in different directions up and down the beach, calling the two boys' names. Nothing.

By 10 p.m., there still was no sign of them, and Eddie and Bruce were positive that something terrible had happened. Jacob and Rodney weren't the best behaved of boys, but they surely knew better than to stay out two hours past curfew.

Feeling he had no choice, Eddie reached for the Amelia Island phone book and dialed the number on the back cover for the local police. His heart raced as he waited for the call to go through.

"Island police," answered the voice on the other line.

"Yes ma'am. I need to report two missing boys."

"When did you last see them?"

"About four hours ago. They were walking on the beach with two young girls, we think."

Eddie gave full descriptions of both boys, then walked back outside to continue his own search. Bruce loaded the other boys into the minivan and drove into town. Returning to the water's edge, Eddie scanned reluctantly down the long strand in each direction looking for anything that might resemble two bodies rolling in the surf.

"Oh, Lord, please help me find them," he prayed. "I should never have let them leave after supper. If they tried wading out into the water, they might have gotten pulled under in an undertow. They don't understand the dangers."

Eddie stood helpless in the chilly surf, his feet and pants legs getting soaked a couple of times. For several minutes of frustration, he couldn't decide whether to stay put or walk along the shoreline again.

"Eddie!"

It was Bruce, yelling over the roaring waves from several yards away at the edge of a sand dune. Eddie launched himself into a full sprint. As he closed in, his heart leapt to his throat at the sight of a police car parked outside the ocean villa beside the minivan.

"They're okay. They're fine," Bruce said, waving his hands in a show of assurance just as Eddie strode beside him.

"What happened?"

Eddie continued to run past Bruce and toward the villa, causing Bruce to spin around and chase after him. "Hold on, Eddie. I said they're okay!" he said, running hard to keep up in the deep sand.

"What's the police car doing here?"

"You gave them our address, and they just happened to pull up

at the same time I got back. I found Jacob and Rodney walking out
of a convenience store back in town with those two girls of theirs."

Eddie stopped dead in his tracks. All of a sudden, he felt his
fear for Jacob and Rodney replaced with intense anger. He forced
himself to calm down long enough to thank the two police officers
and apologize for their trouble. Then, he marched directly inside
the villa to confront the two boys.

Both Jacob and Rodney had brushed their teeth and prepared
for bed, hoping somehow that the effort would count for something.
It didn't.

"Okay, boys. Do either of you have any idea or even care about
all the stress that you have caused us tonight? I just had to apologize to the police department for your irresponsibility."

Neither boy said a word. They had never seen Eddie blow his
top — ever — and it was petrifying. Rodney was sure that Eddie
would take a belt to both of them. They hadn't meant to stay out so
late, but both realized they had crossed the line.

"We're sorry," Rodney said, summoning the courage to speak
first.

"Yeah, we just lost track of time," Jacob said.

"I would think that the sun going down must have given you a
clue that it was getting late," Eddie said. "Do you boys realize that
if something had happened to you, it probably would have ruined
everything we've worked for at Eagle Ranch?"

Eddie stormed out of the room, leaving the boys to contemplate
their show of poor judgment.

"Those girls weren't worth it, were they?" Jacob said several
seconds after the door shut behind Eddie.

"Nope."

"Hey, do you think Eddie's going to whip us?"

"I reckon he will — big time."

But Eddie never returned to their room that night, and in the
morning, he didn't say a word about the incident until they were in
the van halfway up the interstate toward home.

"Jacob, Rodney, ... when we get back to the ranch, I'll have a long list of chores for you to do as punishment for breaking curfew. And that's all I'm saying about this whole affair for now. We do our best to help you guys. But in the end, it's up to you whether you'll make something of yourselves. … By the way, I'm sorry I lost my temper back there."

Rodney and Jacob, joined by the rest of the boys who felt guilty by association, stared down in silence at the floorboard of the van. Their dispirited calm was a noticeable contrast to the buzz of excitement that filled the vehicle three days earlier on the way down. Rodney's mind whirled in confusion. He still couldn't understand why his misbehavior had not warranted an all-out beating. Until he came to Eagle Ranch, every man in his life had beaten and bruised him for any number of transgressions. And now, here he had screwed up the most since coming to the ranch, and despite his obvious anger, Eddie still had not come close to whipping him.

Rodney looked across the seat at Jacob's face and wondered if he was thinking the same thing. They had let Eddie down — and that hurt a whole lot worse than any beating.

Chapter Thirty-Two

Eagle Ranch celebrated its first Christmas in 1985. Three of the boys, including Rodney, had remained at the Faith Home. Two had nowhere to go home to, but Rodney's reason for staying at the ranch was of his own making. He had continued to shut out his mother, and Sally Hudgins had all but given up. Since October, she had not shown up for the last four scheduled meetings at the ranch, and she no longer called. Her only recent contact with the ranch had been through the mail with a signed permission slip for Rodney's trip to Amelia Island. Bruce's numerous efforts to contact her by phone had been unsuccessful.

Rodney had not asked about his mother's estrangement or even indicated that he cared. Nevertheless, he continued to make progress in his development at the ranch. Since returning from the fiasco at Amelia Island, he and Jacob had not complained once about their long list of overtime duties — clearing brush, laying sod, and scores of other necessary chores. Eddie was a perfectionist in regard to any job at the ranch, especially those affecting the property's outward appearance, and he was pleased with the fruits of the boys' hard labor.

Christmas Day was a welcome break, for Rodney found that despite his continued workouts for wrestling, all the yard work made his muscles sorer. It was nice to have a day off. Tony and Trish went out of their way to make the best Christmas ever for the boys who remained at the ranch. Each boy had a stocking full of treats and several presents under the live Fraser fir in the living room of the Faith Home. By noontime, a messy collection of assorted toys and shredded wrapping paper of red and green lay scattered throughout every corner of the room. All three boys, along with the Dittmeiers' own two children, sat on the floor, eating chocolates and perusing through each other's booty of gifts.

Noticing the fire in the fireplace beginning to wane, Tony stood up from the scene to step outside for more wood. As he opened the front door and scooted out into the brisk air, something knocked against his right shoe. Crouching down, he picked up a small box crudely wrapped in tissue paper and a green ribbon bow. The paper felt cold to his touch, so he figured it must have been there for some time. Turning over the present, he spotted a small tag on the bottom. Scribbled in red ink was Rodney's name.

"Hey, Trish. I think you left one of Rodney's gifts out here — unless it came from Santa!"

Walking back inside, Tony handed the present to Rodney, who was seated on the floor beside Trish.

"That's not from us, Tony," Trish said, looking confused. "But go ahead, Rodney … open it up!"

Rodney took the present and carefully tore away the thin paper from a flimsy white box. As he lifted off the top, Trish nudged her chin against the back of his shoulder to peek at what was inside. It was a black imitation crocodile-skin wallet.

"Wow! That's really nice," Trish said.

Rodney spread open the two sides of the billfold and removed another tag from inside. Like the other card, something had been written in red ink. Rodney stood up, dropping the gift along with the card to the floor, and walked upstairs to his room without a word.

Puzzled, Tony looked at his wife with questioning eyes. She reached down to the floor to retrieve the small card and held it up for her husband to see. The simple inscription read, "Love, Mama."

✛ ✛ ✛

In January, following the end of Christmas holidays, the wrestling season resumed at Johnson High, and Rodney continued to train with the varsity. He was even allowed to dress out with the team for competitions held at home. Although he had not wrestled in a match, it was a proud feeling to stand alongside his older teammates on the mat. Among the varsity boys, there were whispers about Rodney's difficult upbringing, and the knowledge seemed to endear him to them. Rodney became the team's adopted younger brother.

Midway into the season, Rodney reported one afternoon to practice to learn that the senior boy who wrestled ahead of him in the 103-pound weight class had separated his shoulder in a hard fall to the mat. A doctor advised the injured wrestler to sit out the next several days; he would have to miss the important upcoming match against North Gwinnett on Friday night. The coach promptly announced to the team that Rodney would make his first start in the senior's place.

Following the ensuing hour-long practice, Coach Doug Thurmond pulled Rodney aside, sitting down beside him on one of the wooden bleacher seats as the rest of the team filed toward the locker room. "How do you feel, son?"

"I don't know what to think. I didn't think I'd get to wrestle in a real match until next season."

"Well, let me tell you something that you probably already know — or at least you should. Your opponent Friday is a senior who has been to the state finals twice. Placed third his first year, and second the next. I expect he'll go all the way this year."

"Yes sir, I know all about him."

"I don't like to tell my boys that they can't win. But in this case, Rodney, I don't want you to get your hopes up. You just get in there, wrestle your best, and I'll be proud. That guy graduates after this season. You'll get your shot next year. Understood?"

"Yeah."

"Okay, go hit the showers. Good workout today."

Rodney walked in slow, measured steps toward the dressing room. Across his tiny shoulders, he carried the double weight of excitement and pending doom. He could hardly wait till Friday, and he could hardly wait till it was over.

✛ ✛ ✛

Word spread fast at the ranch, and preparations were made for all staff and boys to attend Rodney's first varsity wrestling match. Rodney pretended to enjoy the outpouring of praise and support, but deep inside he dreaded the thought of humiliating himself in front of his closest friends.

Eddie continued to be concerned about Rodney's mother. He and Bruce still had been unable to reach her by phone. Surely she would want to see her son wrestle on Friday night. It would be a proud moment for any parent. On the Thursday evening before the match, after several more unsuccessful calls during the day, he made up his mind to visit her himself. Somehow, he had to let her know.

Driving up to the mobile home park in Buford that night, Eddie scanned the long row of thin-metal structures until he found Number 3-A. He checked his notebook to confirm the address, then pulled his Toyota up to the front door. He was in luck. Inside, a light was on.

A skinny, bearded man wearing jeans and a black-smudged T-shirt answered the door suspiciously. "What do you want?" he asked, glaring at Eddie through a cracked door that was still chain-locked on the inside. "I ain't making no more plumbing calls tonight."

"I was looking for Sally Hudgins."

"What do you want with her?"

"I'm sorry. I'm Eddie Staub. I help take care of her son, Rodney, at Eagle Ranch. We've been trying to call her for several weeks but haven't gotten an answer."

"Phone's been out, and I ain't got around to getting the phone company out here. They'll just rip me off, anyway."

"Is Sally here?"

"Nope."

"Could you tell me where she is?"

"Over at the diner, downtown. She's been working double-shift all month."

"Thanks. Sorry to have bothered you tonight."

"It's okay."

Eddie hopped back in his car and drove the three miles into town. He quickly found the brightly lighted 24-hour restaurant where Sally worked. Inside, Rodney's mother was waiting on a table in the back. Spotting an empty bar stool near the cash register, he plopped down on the seat and waited. She finished taking an order and quickly scooted toward a row of coffee pots toward the front of the restaurant.

"Sally," Eddie called out as she walked by.

She stopped, looking back over her shoulder. Having never seen Eddie outside the ranch, she appeared not to recognize him at first. Her mouth opened and her mind spun. Finally, she remembered and a look of worry spread across her face.

"Is something wrong with Rodney?"

"No. He's fine. We just hadn't heard from you in so long. I've tried to call, but I understand your phone's been out."

"Yeah, it has."

"I was hoping you could visit the ranch soon to see your son. I'm sure he'd love to see you."

"Has he asked to see me?"

"Well …"

"Then I don't care to see him either."

"Wait a minute, Sally."

"Order up!" a voice yelled from the kitchen.

"I'm sorry, I've got to get back to work."

"Wait, one more minute, I promise. I've got some good news. Rodney made the varsity wrestling team, and he's going to be wrestling in his first match tomorrow night at the Johnson High gym.

Since he's just a freshman, no one expects him to win. But it's still quite an accomplishment, and I thought you might like to be there."

"I've got to work that night. But thanks for telling me," she said, walking back toward the kitchen.

Oh well, Eddie thought, sliding off the stool. At least I tried.

✛ ✛ ✛

The blanket of powder-blue mats provided a soft touch to the scarred tartan floor of the Johnson High School gym and a paradoxical backdrop to the Friday night wrestling match between Johnson and North Gwinnett. In the stands, Eddie sat next to Bruce about seven rows up, high enough to see over the constant flow of students but close enough for a bird's-eye view of center court. The two had come to the gym a half-hour early to claim their perch and reserve several more seats for Rodney's Eagle Ranch "fan club."

If Eddie and Bruce had been slated to wrestle instead of Rodney, they could not have felt any more nervous than they did at that moment. Close by, a small ensemble of the Johnson High School band began warming up, and both men felt the drums pushing their heartbeats to keep up with the rhythm. Along with the loudening hum of the building crowd of adults and students, the whole scene took on a feel of being larger than life. Trying to keep his perspective, Eddie told himself over and over that it was just a game, a little scuffle between boys. At least that's what his head said — his pounding heart obviously wasn't buying it.

"Quit that," Eddie said, nudging Bruce with an elbow. Bruce was sitting on his hands, rocking back and forth and humming tight-lipped to the band music. "You're making me nervous."

"I'm making *you* nervous?" Bruce said.

"Just kidding. …You know, I don't think I'm going to be able to watch this thing."

"I know what you mean."

"He's worked so hard," Eddie said. "I just hope he's not humiliated out there."

"Yeah, poor guy — he gets his first shot to prove something and it's against a guy picked to win the state tournament," Bruce said.

"It doesn't seem fair, does it?"

"I wish this crowd wasn't so big. Look at all these people! Wrestling sure wasn't this big back when I was in high school."

Bruce suddenly eyed Tony and Trish with their entourage of boys in tow on the opposite side of the gym. Standing, he waved until they noticed him, then sat back down on his hands. By the time they made it to their seats, the gym's mechanical scoreboard sounded its horn, indicating the start of the tournament.

Rodney would wrestle first, which possibly explained why much of the crowd still talked and milled about. The more interesting matchups would follow. At least we'll get it over with, Eddie figured.

A scorekeeper turned on his microphone to welcome the crowd, then announced the names of Rodney and his opponent.

"Here we go," Bruce said, still rocking.

The two boys walked to the middle of the mat and shook hands. The referee placed a hand across each boy's shoulders, mumbling a few brief instructions and encouraging them to be good sports. Then he positioned them a few feet apart, simultaneously plugging his mouth with a silver whistle. Both youths immediately crouched into a set position.

"Go, Rodney!" Trish yelled, standing up and clapping her hands. A few heads around her turned and smiled as her husband feigned mild embarrassment.

On the mat, Rodney didn't hear her shouts. He didn't hear anything or anyone. He was consumed in total concentration, waiting for the whistle. In front of him, the lanky opponent chomped hungrily on a clear plastic mouthpiece. Holding one hand high in the air, the referee stole a quick glance at the scoreboard clock high above a basketball goal on the north end of the gym. "2:00" was posted in bright electric yellow. Eddie drew in a big breath and held it. Everyone and everything on the court were frozen … and then the hand came down with a short spurt from the whistle.

The two boys came out of their crouch and began circling, faking and bobbing their heads left and right, each looking for an opening. The experienced state wrestler found it first, latching onto Rodney's shoulders and twisting him down hard to the blue mat. Like a tiger, he pounced quickly atop his prey and began working his hands in pretzel-like motions until finding a secure hold. With powerful precision, he spun Rodney off his knees and onto his back. Only twenty seconds had expired.

"Oh no!" Trish moaned, still on her feet as she covered her mouth with one hand.

"I can't watch this," said Eddie, looking away briefly to check the clock.

"Me either," said Bruce. He rocked faster.

Rodney curled his back and pushed up with all his might. His left shoulder was pinned, and he strained to prevent the other from touching and ending the match. The referee went down on all fours, pressing his head sideways to the spongy mat to monitor the slowly waning crack of light between Rodney's shoulder and the floor. Rodney twisted, momentarily buying a little more airspace, and then losing it just as quickly. His opponent, sensing victory, tightened every muscle and pressed on with increased fury. Rodney strained with everything he had to break free but found himself paralyzed. He was like a fly locked in a spider's final death grip, buzzing and vibrating but going nowhere.

Another thirty seconds went by, and the boy on top apparently grew restless. He released his hold for a quarter-second, then slid his arms into a new position. Rodney hardly had time to react, but he managed to scoot his body slightly to one side. His legs scrambled free, and he frantically shifted them back and forth against the mat. The motion sent the two boys spinning in place.

The home crowd, most of them having found their seats, cheered as the match began to pique their interest. The freshman underdog may be down on points, but he was holding off a superior state-class wrestler after a full ninety seconds.

Eddie, Bruce, Tony, Trish, and the boys all shouted their encouragement. Their heads ticked back and forth, glancing at the clock and then back to the mat like an out-of-synch crowd at a tennis match.

"C'mon Rodney, c'mon," Eddie urged under his breath. "You can do it, buddy. Just a few more seconds. C'mon. C'mon. C'mon…" His hands gripped the bleacher seat tighter and tighter until he felt the muscles in his forearms begin to burn with ten seconds to go.

Rodney strained harder, sensing he wouldn't have to for much longer. But he felt himself growing weaker. His opponent grunted and snorted in desperate competition with the clock. Rodney's free shoulder sank lower and lower … and finally the buzzer sounded. Both of Rodney's shoulders immediately touched the mat. One second more and he would have been pinned.

The bleachers on both sides went berserk, stomping and cheering as if Rodney had won the match. The older boy jumped to his feet. He shouted and slapped his hands in frustration. Then he began walking around and around in tiny circles, muttering to himself as Rodney lay on his back, exhausted.

"Isn't he great? Isn't he great!" Trish said, bouncing excitedly. Her eyes were wet with emotion.

Eddie felt a momentary release of tension and sat back down. Even Bruce had stopped his nervous ritual. Tony put one arm around Trish and the other around Jacob to his left. They all felt tired, and the brief intermission gave them little time to recover.

The referee signaled for the boys to return and take their places. Rodney crouched onto his hands and knees. His opponent, wiggling his arms to stay loose, walked back to the mat and huddled over his young competitor in the superior position. Rodney felt the boy grab his left elbow, then slide an arm around his waist. Both boys looked up at the referee. The crowd hushed and waited, then erupted with the whistle. Almost immediately, Rodney was on his back again. A collective "oh" sounded from the bleachers.

The next two minutes resembled the first, with Rodney squirming and straining under his opponent's relentless attack. But even from seven rows back, Eddie could see plenty of fight left in Rodney's dark brown eyes. All his life had been spent on his back;

only now, he was fighting back. It was as if, for the first time, he truly believed in himself.

The horn sounded an end to the second period, and still Rodney had refused to give in. Both boys appeared drained as they stood up much more slowly than before. Still breathing hard, Rodney stepped over to his team's side of the mat where he was immediately surrounded by the other wrestlers.

"Let him breathe, let him breathe!" Coach Thurmond shouted, pulling the boys apart. In the middle, Rodney stood hunched over, his hands gripping the bottom cuffs of his blue uniform shorts for support. The coach tried to offer advice, barking only a few inches from his left ear in an attempt to be heard over the reverberating cheers of the gym. But Rodney wasn't listening. He was in another world, staring through his coach and teammates to a distant corner of the gym.

Eddie's eyes focused on the same spot, a darkened doorway below a red-lighted exit sign, at almost the exact second. A woman dressed in a plain white uniform stood there, holding a small pocketbook in both hands. Someone from behind pointed for her to move, and she stepped up onto the first row of the bleachers.

"Bruce, look to my left — down in the corner."

Bruce leaned forward slightly and saw the woman standing alone on the bleacher step.

"Did she just now get here?"

"I'm not sure," Eddie said, "but I'm glad she made it."

Eddie looked back at Rodney and followed his eyes. He, too, had spotted his mother.

✛ ✛ ✛

Despite a few burned-out bulbs, the gym's scoreboard performed an apt job of informing the spectators:

"Period 3. Home 0. Visitor 9."

Rodney would lose on points. But in the crowd's opinion, he won the match if he avoided being pinned. The North Gwinnett wrestler felt the same. Technically, he had the match sewn up, but his pride would settle for nothing less than two shoulders against the mat.

Eddie stared down at his hands and saw the moisture. So this is what they mean by sweaty palms, he thought, smiling tensely. He stood up in his seat, joining the rest of the bleachers crowd, as Rodney returned to the center of the mat for the final period. One-hundred and twenty more seconds.

"C'mon Rodney! You can do it!" Eddie yelled, his voice already starting to sound hoarse.

The entire gym was on its feet, stomping the wooden bleachers with a thundering rumble. It seemed like everyone realized all at once how far this little freshman had come — not just on the mat but in his life. As trite as it sounded, Eddie couldn't help but realize the symbolism. This whole match — three brief periods in time — was really a microcosm of Rodney's entire young life. Heck, it was even bigger than that, Eddie thought. It was illustrative of Eddie's whole struggle the last three years to fulfill his impossible dream. For in Rodney, Eddie saw the hopes of Eagle Ranch.

The whistle blew, and once again the referee went down on his knees to follow the senior as he collapsed on top of Rodney and spun him on his back. Rodney's face was beet-red and his veins glared from beneath the skin of his neck. He pounded his right fist violently to the mat, fighting desperately to keep his free right shoulder from going down. It was close and getting closer. The referee pushed his face in as close as he could to the two boys without touching the tangled heap, closing one eye as he inspected the progress. He raised his hand in the air. It seemed to twitch in anticipation, signaling the end was near.

"This is it, I'm afraid," Eddie muttered. "This is it …"

Rodney opened his mouth in a silent, agonizing scream. His mind told him to push, but his tired body was giving in. And then, with exactly half a period remaining, he felt his straining right shoulder lighten and lift just a little. His opponent's sweaty grip had slipped, if only for a brief second.

It happened again, and this time Rodney reacted. He quickly

formed a defensive bridge with his body. Then, in a move occurring so fast that most people in the stands missed it, Rodney flipped his opponent with a flawless reversal move. For the first time in the match, Rodney was on top.

The crowd, which had all but given up on the freshman, roared back to life. Rodney slid one arm around his stunned opponent's waist and placed the other across the boy's chest. And then he pushed and pushed with every last morsel of strength in his body. He pushed and pushed until both shoulders of the older boy firmly met the mat. The referee's hand slapped the floor with a loud crack, and every muscle in Rodney's body collapsed at once. The referee reached over the two expended bodies, taking hold of Rodney's limp right arm and raising it high for all the crowd to see.

Rodney Hudgins was a winner.

✦ ✦ ✦

Eddie felt the lump growing bigger in his throat as he stood watching the celebration on the gym floor. He tried to freeze the scene in his mind, savoring the moment while it lasted. Tony, Trish, and Bruce hugged each other, the boys, and even a few strangers in the stands.

On the mat, Rodney surfaced from beneath a deep pile of his teammates. With a look of exhaustion, but wearing a broad smile, he limped toward the bleachers where his Eagle Ranch family stood waiting.

"Way to go, buddy!" Eddie said, tousling Rodney's wet head of hair, then standing back as Bruce and the others fielded a round of high-fives.

"Eddie, are you proud of me?"

"I sure am. ... I'm very proud of you," he said, squeezing Rodney's shoulders with a one-armed hug.

Rodney looked to his right down the long row of bleachers, then stared down at his feet, biting his bottom lip.

"She's here," he said, sounding uneasy.

"I know," Eddie said. "She got here just in time."

Rodney pulled away from Eddie's grasp and walked slowly

across the top of the sixth row toward his mother. Seeing his approach, Sally Hudgins stood up from her seat and waited, smiling nervously.

"You looked real good out there," she said as he stepped up beside her.

"Thanks."

An awkward silence hung between them as each struggled for something more to say. After a whole life together, it had taken only a few months to make a mother and son feel like strangers.

"I'm so proud of you, Rodney. Could you … give me a hug?"

"I'm pretty sweaty right now, Mama."

She smiled, brushing back a strand of hair. Her eyes started to moisten with tears.

"I don't mind," she said, her voice breaking on the last syllable.

Four aisles away, Eddie and Bruce watched the two figures embrace, and together felt the same feeling at the same time.

"Seeing that makes me feel like Rodney just might make it," Bruce said. His arms folded across his chest as wave after wave of satisfaction bathed his entire body.

Eddie stuffed his hands slowly inside the front pockets of his jeans. "Yeah, it sure feels like a good start."

PICTORIAL EPILOGUE

Eddie Staub is interviewed by WSB-TV reporter David Johnson in 1983. The race to raise $144,000 in 120 days attracted local and national publicity.

Living on a diet of cheese and crackers in order to save money, Eddie Staub lost over thirty pounds during his early fund-raising efforts on behalf of the ranch.

A jubilant spirit was evident at the successful land closing for the Eagle Ranch site on August 18, 1983. Pictured with Eddie Staub is Nina Rusk Hosch, co-executrix for the land which was part of her family's trust.

Hall County Commissioner Clara Nunn visits the ranch site after voting to approve its rezoning application. The ranch met with some initial skepticism from surrounding neighbors.

Eddie Staub and members of the Gainesville Kiwanis Club, which donated $20,000 toward ranch construction, break ground. No construction or development ever takes place until all funds are secured. This philosophy has enabled Eagle Ranch to remain debt free.

The first construction at the ranch began in the winter of 1983, a few months after the final dollar was raised for the land purchase. An old barn on the property served as Eddie Staub's first office.

The Eagle Ranch property, pointed out by its original sign, is located in the rural community of Chestnut Mountain in Hall County, Georgia.

The John W. Jacobs Sr. Administration Building was completed in May 1984. It served as Eddie Staub's home for four years.

Christmas is one of Eagle Ranch's many special family traditions. Pictured (from left) are Trish Dittmeier, Eddie Staub, Trish's daughter Emily, and ranch secretary Jean Parks.

The first boys' home, the Faith Home, was completed in April 1985. Each home on the ranch is approximately 5,700 square feet, housing up to seven children and a houseparent couple.

Bruce Burch (left), a former counselor at a highly respected children's treatment center in Atlanta, introduced the therapeutic aspect of the ranch's innovative program.

Gainesville community leader Loyd Strickland (left) and University of Georgia Head Football Coach Vince Dooley are honored at a ranch picnic celebration in 1991. Both men took an early interest and played key roles in the formation of Eagle Ranch.

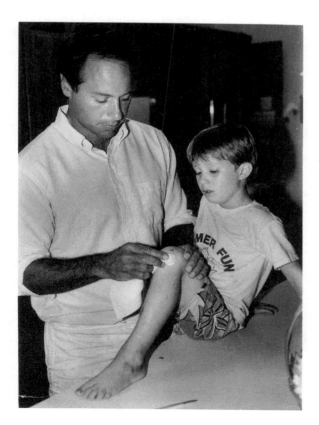

Tony Dittmeier (left) bandaged more than a few scrapes while serving as Eagle Ranch's first houseparent along with his wife, Trish.

Eagle Ranch celebrated its ten-year anniversary in 1995. Funding for the ranch continues to be provided primarily through private donations from individuals, churches, civic clubs, corporations and foundations.

Eagle Ranch is a working farm with horses, cows and even a few dogs and cats. The animals are important to the children's healing process.

Author's Note

Eagle Ranch celebrated its tenth anniversary in April 1995. Since its inception, the operation has touched the lives of more than 100 boys and is widely recognized for its innovative and cutting-edge therapeutic program.

The mission remains the same. Eagle Ranch provides a Christ-centered home for boys ages six to eighteen who have been abused, neglected or who are in need of a stronger family support system. The ranch's goal is the "spiritual, intellectual, emotional, social and physical development" of the children entrusted in its care and the eventual reunification with their natural families whenever possible.

"On Eagle's Wings" is based on a true story gleaned from interviews with the Eagle Ranch founder, staff, friends, supporters, and other contacts. For privacy purposes, the characters and names of Rodney and the boys of Eagle Ranch are not real persons. Although each of their individual stories is based on actual boys who have passed through the doors of the ranch, certain facts may have been changed to avoid potential disclosure of their identities.

This book project was directed by the Eagle Ranch Board of Directors with the intent of providing a written history of the ranch. It is dedicated to all the boys of Eagle Ranch — past, present and future. May God bless them.